El Boffo Buffo . . .

That's Italian for "the big laugh" . . . and
here is the ultimate collection of the funniest,
silliest, newest, most inane, ridiculous, ir-
reverent, and hilarious Italian humor ever.
Which should make everybody happy . . .
especially the Italians.

This is absolutely the last side-splitting
word on the world's best Italian jokes, and
we dare you to flip these pages and not be
caught up in an infectious fit of laughter at
the zany antics of these Raucous Romans,
Sexy Sicilians, and Naughty Neapolitans.

It's wildly contagious, and will leave you
laughing . . . even if you're not Italian.

Books by Larry Wilde

MORE The Official Democrat/Republican Joke Book
MORE The Official Smart Kids/Dumb Parents Joke Book
The Official Book of Sick Jokes
MORE The Official Jewish/Irish Joke Book
The LAST Official Italian Joke Book
The Official Cat Lovers/Dog Lovers Joke Book
The Official Dirty Joke Book
The LAST Official Polish Joke Book
The Official Golfers Joke Book
The Official Smart Kids/ Dumb Parents Joke Book
The Official Religious/NOT SO Religious Joke Book
The Official Democrat/Republican Joke Book
MORE The Official Polish/Italian Joke Book
The Official Black Folks/White Folks Joke Book
The Official Virgins/Sex Maniacs Joke Book
The Official Jewish/Irish Joke Book
The Official Polish/Italian Joke Book
The Official Bedroom/Bathroom Joke Book

also

The Complete Book of Ethnic Humor (Corwin)
How The Great Comedy Writers Create Laughter
   (Nelson-Hall)
The Great Comedians (Citadel Press)

The Last Official Italian Joke Book

By Larry Wilde

PINNACLE BOOKS • NEW YORK

THE *LAST* OFFICIAL ITALIAN JOKE BOOK

An original Pinnacle Books edition, published for the first time anywhere.

First printing, November 1978
Second printing, July 1979
Third printing, October 1979
Fourth printing, January 1981
Fifth printing, August 1981
Sixth printing, May 1982

ISBN: 0-523-41970-8

Cover illustration by Ron Wing

Printed in the United States of America

PINNACLE BOOKS, INC.
1430 Broadway
New York, New York 10018

This book is affectionately dedicated to Christopher Columbus, the world's first wheeler-dealer:

He didn't know where he was going. When he got there he didn't know where he was. When he got back he didn't know where he had been. And he did it all on borrowed money.

About the Author

The LAST Official Italian Joke Book represents a milestone in the remarkably versatile career of Larry Wilde. With the sale of over 3,500,000 books, *author* Larry Wilde is now America's number one best-selling humorist.

Comedian Larry Wilde has been making people laugh for over 25 years in the nation's leading hotels and night clubs, while *actor* Larry Wilde is seen on television in commercials and situation comedy series.

Larry was born under the sign of Aquarius in Jersey City, New Jersey. After a two-year hitch in the United States Marine Corps he received his bachelor of arts degree at the University of Miami, Florida.

In addition to the *Official* joke book series, Mr. Wilde has also published two serious works dealing with the technique of humor: *The Great Comedians* (Citadel) *and How the Great Comedy Writers Create Laughter* (Nelson-Hall).

The author's newest contribution to the comedic art form is a hardcover collection of jokes representing over twenty minority groups: *The Complete Book of Ethnic Humor* (Corwin Books).

Mr. Wilde is married to the former Maryruth Poulos of Hanna, Wyoming. The couple reside in Los Angeles, California.

Contents

The 1st Official

Italian Joke Book

INTRODUCTION

Several years ago, when *The Official Polish/Italian Joke Book* was published (half the book contained Polish jokes; the other half Italian jokes) a series of rather unusual incidents took place.

In Detroit, the book was burned at a rally by two college students who protested the publishing of Polish jokes.

In Buffalo, a Polish newspaper blasted the book and begged its readers not to buy it.

From Cleveland and Chicago came protest letters by Polish groups (not one from an Italian organization).

But the crowning event took place in Los Angeles, California.

A Polish man, angered by the book's contents, entered a department store, removed dozens of copies of *The Polish/Italian Joke Book* from display and tore off the Polish side of the book. After ripping it to shreds, he placed the Italian side back on the shelf ready to be sold. (The episode was covered in the *Los Angeles Times*.)

Obviously, the gentleman was hypersensitive and overreacted. But, interestingly, to this Pole, jokes about Italians were perfectly acceptable. Of course, his action also underscored a generally accepted fact: *Italians can take a joke.*

Witness the humor expressed by comedian Pat Henry. Pat is of Italian descent, and with great love he kids his own people:

> *There was once a banquet organized to protest discrimination against Italian-Americans. What shrewd planning that was. The dais alone represented eight hundred years off for good behavior.*

Obviously, you don't have to be Italian to kid Italians. What you have to have is a comic spirit. This is the wit of the well-liked black funnyman, Nipsey Russell:

> *We don't mess with Italians because it's just too hard to sing 'We Shall Overcome' with a mouthful of cement.*

2

The comedians in Las Vegas recognize that their audiences contain many Italians from all over America and, therefore, cater to their comedy tastes. Here are some boffs delivered by the popular Dave Barry:

If you want to learn to speak Italian all you need to know is one word:

Atsa!
Atsa table, atsa chair . . .

Rafferty and Gigliani were working on a construction job. "My brotha just-a had-a da twins," announced Gigliani. "A boy and a girl."
"Now that's nice ta hear," replied the Irishman. "What did they call the girl?"
"Denise!" answered Gigliani.
"And what about the boy?"
"Da nephew!" said the Italian proudly.

One of the most admired Italian comedians is Pasquale Caputo, better known as Pat Cooper. He could easily be the Italian version of Sam Levenson, for Pat has evoked enormous laughter from crowds with his childhood recollections:

3

We had 45 religious statues in our house. It was pretty spooky. I mean, how would you like to have 90 eyes staring at you every time you sat down to eat?

Jim Bishop, the erudite author and newspaper columnist, once wrote a column in which he stated that "good comics get their material from acts of cruelty, frustration, and humiliation." He then cited a line delivered by the brilliant café comic, Shecky Greene:

Frank Sinatra once saved my life. I was being beaten to death by four gangsters and Sinatra came along. I heard him say, "That's enough!"

Frank Sinatra is affectionately referred to by his colleagues as the "Chairman of the Board." That honorary title is more than justified. It seems to be a general rule in life that the bigger the man the greater his sense of humor. Sinatra has been kidded throughout his entire career, but it appears the more pointed the barbs thrown at him the louder he laughs.

When "Ol' Blue Eyes" was the central figure in a Dean Martin roast, he proved

4

once again that Italians have the ability to gaffaw and with good grace. Get a gander at some of the zingers:

Orson Welles called him the "Godfather of show business."

Don Rickles: *Frank's best friend couldn't be here—he's on a hook in New Jersey.*

Dean Martin: *Frank lent money to New York. When they didn't repay, he broke the Statue of Liberty's arms.*

Milton Berle: *This is a great crowd. I was going to say mob— but you know how sensitive Frank is.*
Half of Frank's pals couldn't be here. Half couldn't find the time and the other half are doing time.
But Frank's the king. He speaks to God on a one-to-one basis. He's so big, he wears a cross with nobody on it.
Frank calls Dial-a-Prayer to see if he has any messages.

Watching Sinatra roar with laughter at

the roasting by his contemporaries, it becomes obvious that he is the consummate example of the Italian "sunny disposition." The Irish, Jewish, and black sense of humor is often mentioned as a recognizable ethnic trait but, unquestionably, Italians should also share that recognition.

The following pages represent the worst and the best of the current Italian gags. They also represent the healthy Roman attitude toward humor and once again prove that *Italians can take a joke.*

Asalud!

RAUCOUS ROMANS

Candolli, on a trans-Atlantic flight from Rome, was carrying on a loud conversation with the stewardess. He wanted the other passengers to be impressed with his English. Candolli asked the hostess, "How high is this plane?"

"Nineteen thousand feet," she answered.

"Oh?" said the Italian, "How wide is it?"

*   *   *

The manager of the symphony orchestra looked up at Razozzi, the applicant. He observed the Italian's green checked jacket and his long black mustache.

"And what was your previous occupation?" he asked.

"I was an organist," exclaimed Razozzi.

"Why did you give that up?" questioned the manager.

"The monkey he's-a die," replied the Italian.

Labanchi, the oversexed movie producer from Rome, arrived in Hollywood. He interviewed a beautiful young actress for the lead in his new picture. "You just-a right," he told her. "Right-a face, right-a voice, coloring right, just-a what's called for in-a da script. Tell-a me, you married?"

"Yes."

"Sorry," snapped the producer. "You too tall."

Zarini: I hear you're gonna marry Grazia Maria. Don't do it! Everybody in Yonkers has had her.

Murano: So, is Yonkers such a big city?

* * *

What do they call an Italian geologist in Georgia?

A dirty wop.

* * *

Miss Petruzzi was out with a young Air Force lieutenant when the familiar sound of aircraft engines overhead made them look up.

"That's a mailplane," announced the airman.

"Beats me how you can tell at this distance," said the Italian girl.

* * *

Why do Mafia hit men never indulge in sexual foreplay?

They're afraid of injuring their trigger fingers.

Is an I.Q. of 156 considered high?
Yes!
For seven Italians?

* * *

In London, Lady Ashcroft decided to give a snooty party, and hired a maid, Miss Scapeccia, who had recently migrated to England.

"Now don't forget the sugar tongs," ordered the English matron. "It's not very nice when the men go in the loo, and they take themselves out, and they put themselves back, and then they have to pick up the sugar lumps with their fingers."

"Yes-a, ma'am," answered the Italian girl.

Later that night, after the guests had gone, Lady Ashcroft said, "Miss Scapeccia, I thought I told you about the sugar tongs!"

"I put-a them out, Lady. I swear!"

"Well, I didn't see them on the table!"

"On-a da table? No! I put-a them in-a da toilet."

Mrs. Zarrelli got caught in the rain while wearing her new Easter hat. She pulled the back of her skirt up over her head to protect the hat and ran for cover.

Tegolini spotted her and began laughing. "Hey, Missus, you ass is-a stickin' out-a three feet!"

"I know it!" she replied, "but that ass is-a-fifty-five years old, and this-a hat is-a brand new!"

13

How do Italians count money?

1, 2, 3, 4, 5, another, another, another . . .

* * *

Did you hear about the rich Italian family who sent their son to summer camp?

The boy wrote home that he'd grown another foot, so Mama knitted him another sock.

* * *

Why won't an Italian ever be elected President of the United States?

They'll never find enough linoleum to cover all the floors in the White House.

* * *

Rasconi and Tavazzi went behind a hedge to pee. "I wish I had a big one like my brother," announced Rasconi. "His is so big he has to hold it with four fingers."

"But, wait," said Tavazzi, "you're holding yours with four fingers!"

"Yeah, but I'm wetting on three of them."

One morning farmer Banzetti and Luisa, his youngest daughter, went to town on their horse and cart to do some shopping and sell two piglets. They sold the pigs, bought a sack of flour, and were heading home. Suddenly, Banzetti and Luisa were set on by robbers. The men took everything, including the farmer's watch. "We're ruined, we're ruined," moaned Banzetti.

"No, Father, we're not," said the girl, "we've still got the pig money, I hid it."

"You hid it? But they stripped you!"

"I know, but I stuffed all the bills up my you-know-what."

"Oh, it's-a too bad you Mama no come. We could-a saved the sack of flour, too!"

*　　*　　*

Wilson settled himself and let Bandini, the barber, put the towel around him.

"Before we start," said Wilson, "I know the weather's awful. I don't care who wins the next big fight, and I don't bet on the horse races. I know I'm getting thin on top but I don't mind. Now get on with it!"

"Okay, mista, if you no mind," said the Italian, "I be able to concentrate-a better if you no talk-a so much!"

Amelia was a manicurist in a barber shop. One night, Martin, a rich customer, invited her to dinner. All night they held hands. Then she absentmindedly put his hand in his champagne glass.

* * *

Ninetti and Scappa were in a barber shop, having their hair cut. When Ninetti saw the barber start to sprinkle hair tonic on him, he exclaimed, "Hey! No put-a that stinky stuff on-a me. My wife'll think I smell like-a whorehouse."

"You can put it on-a me," said Scappa. "My wife-a doesn't know what-a whorehouse smells like."

* * *

A man rushed into Pascanti's barber shop and asked, "How many ahead of me?"

"Two haircuts," said Pascanti. The man rushed out but never came back. The next Saturday, he did the same thing. The third Saturday, when the fellow dashed in, Pascanti said, "Three ahead of you. Say . . ." but the fellow was gone. Then Pascanti said to Jackson the shoeshine boy, "You foll-a that man and find out who he is. This is the third time he's-a run in, ask-a how many ahead-a him, then he run out and no come back."

Ten minutes later Jackson returned. "Boss," he said. "Ah doan' know who dat fella is, but ah sho' know where he went!"

"Where?" asked the Italian.

"To yoah house!"

*　　*　　*

A customer was complaining to Santorelli, the barber, about the price of haircuts. "I'm just got back from London," said the man. "Over there I got a good haircut for three dollars."

"Yeah," said the barber, "But look at the fare."

*　　*　　*

His brother-in-law had just come over from Italy, so Gambutti gave him a job in the barber shop. The first morning Gambutti whispered, "Here comes a man for a shave."

"Let-a me practice on-a him."

"Okay," said the barber. "But-a be careful and don' cut-a yourself."

Tommy Leonetti, the talented singing star and motion picture composer, tells this tantalizing tale:

Reverend Baxter dropped into Bennelli's barber shop for a quick shave. Unfortunately, Bennelli was suffering from a terrible hangover. His breath nearly wiped out the poor minister. and on top of that he took a huge nick out of the clergyman's cheek.

"You see," said the minister, as the blood flowed down his face. "what comes from drinking intoxicating liquor?"

"Yeah," said the barber, "It makes-a da skin very tender."

"Da skin is-a very tender!"

Grant was sitting in the barber chair getting a haircut. Fugoni said to him, "You takin' a vacation this year?"

"Yes, my wife and I are flying to Rome tomorrow for a couple of weeks."

"How you goin'?" asked the barber.

"By Pan Am," replied the customer.

"Donna go Pan Am. The food is-a lousy, the stewardesses is ugly, it'll be-a rough all the way. Where you stayin' in-a Roma?"

"At the Hilton," replied Grant.

"Donna stay there. The food is-a no good, the beds are hard, you no get-a good service. What-a you gonna do in Roma?"

"We thought we'd try to get an audience with the Pope."

"Hey, donna waste-a you time. You never get-a near him. There gonna be ten thousand Italians in-a the square smellin' from garlic. You wish you never went near the place."

Grant paid his bill and left. Three weeks later he was back. "Did-a you go to Italy?" asked Fugoni.

"Yep."

"How you go?"

"We went by Pan Am. It was a wonderful trip. The food was excellent, the service was great, and the stewardesses were very pretty."

"Where you stay?" asked the barber.

"At the Hilton. The food was terrific, the beds were the best I've ever slept in, and everybody was marvelous."

"You get-a to see the Pope?"

"Yes. We spent thirty minutes with him. There were only about six people and we didn't have to wait over five minutes. It was one of the highlights of the trip."

"What-a he have-a to say?"

"As I knelt at his feet to receive his blessing, he looked at me and said, "For heaven's sake, where did you get that awful haircut?"

* * *

In the middle of shaving a customer, Nicolanti said, "Mista, you have-a ketchup for-a lunch?"

"No," answered the man.

"Then," said the barber, "I just-a cut-a you throat!"

Did you hear about the Italian girl who couldn't tell which way the elevator was going even though they gave her two guesses?

* * *

What is an Italian sophisticate?
A guy who chews gum after eating garlic.

* * *

Roberto was complaining to his friend Onofrio, "This match won't light!"
"What's-a matta with it?"
"I donna know," said Roberto, "It lit-a before!"

* * *

How do you prepare an Italian cocktail?
Drop a meatball in a glass of wine.

* * *

What do you get if you cross a retarded Puerto Rican with a baboon?
An Italian intellectual.

"Listen, you're Italian, maybe you can tell me what makes the Tower of Pisa lean?"

"If I know I'd-a take some myself," said the 300-pound Mrs. Fachetti.

* * *

"The Jews and the Italians will always be friends. The Jews need the Italians and the Italians need the Jews."

"Why do you say that?"

"It was an Italian who invented the toilet seat. It was a Jew who figured out how to put a hole in it."

* * *

Raymond took his date to a romantic Italian restaurant in Greenwich Village. When the check arrived, Raymond pulled out his wallet and turned beet red.

He called the waiter over. "Look, I'm really very sorry," Raymond said with sincere embarrassment, "I've got just the right amount of cash to cover the check with nothing left over for a tip!"

"Donju worry," said the waiter, "I'm-a gonna just add up-a check once more!"

What is the dirtiest four-letter word in the Italian language?

Work.

* * *

Did you hear about the Italian who quit his job because he was selling baby carriages and the boss gave him virgin territory?

* * *

Sartini stalked into a police station and told the desk sergeant he wanted to swear out a complaint against a truck driver for assault and battery.

"What happened?" asked the bored cop.

"I was in a phone booth and this creep came along and wanted to use the phone," explained Sartini, "I told him to wait a while, but he wouldn't. Finally he slammed open the door and yanked me out of there."

"No wonder you got mad," agreed the sergeant.

"Damn right, I got mad," said the Italian. "The sonuvabitch didn't even give my girlfriend time to put her panties on."

A man having dinner in Canzini's Restaurant called his waiter over. "This soup is cold. Bring me some that's hot."

"What-a you want me do?" said the waiter. "Burn-a my thumb?"

* * *

Impatient Customer: I get only an hour for lunch.

Waiter: I no can talk-a 'bout labor troubles with-a you now.

* * *

Why won't there ever be an Italian First Lady in the White House?

Because they'll never find enough plastic slipcovers for all the furniture.

* * *

What's the Italian word for refrigerator?

Ice-a box.

* * *

What's the Italian word for woman?

Nice-a box.

Mark Harris, the super salesman at Carroll's posh Beverly Hills haberdashery, gets customers howling at this hunk of hyperbole:

Nuvoli and Carlino met one day in the park:

"You make-a lots-a money now?" asked Nuvoli.

"Yeah, I ain't-a doin' too bad!" replied Carlino.

"What-a you gonna do with all-a you money?"

"I'm gonna do something I wanna do my whole-a life."

"What's-a that?"

"I'm-a gonna get me a Polack gardener."

*   *   *

Mrs. Occhilini approached a sales clerk in the department store and asked, "'Sucusa me, can-a you tell me how do I get-a to da ladies' room?"

"Escalator," replied the clerk.

"Oh, no!" said the Italian woman, "I must-a go now!"

Bartoli went to the seashore for his vacation. While he was swimming, a baby shark swam up and chewed off one of Bartoli's toes. When he finally reached the beach, Bartoli stammered out the news to the lifeguard, who rushed over yelling, "Which one?"

"How should I know?" asked the Italian. "One-a shark looks like-a 'notha to me."

* * *

Clarence Pine, the most popular customer relations representative at Los Angeles's Farmers Market, relates this rollicking classic:

Enrico Caruso was the matinee idol of the society opera world in the early 1900s. He was also privately one of the more active lovers of his time. The following remark is attributed to the great Italian tenor.

"I never make love in the morning," said Caruso. "It's bad for the voice; it's bad for the health; and, besides, you never know who you might meet in the afternoon."

Jack Rosenbaum, the stalwart sales veep for California's CFS Continental, savors this spirit lifter:

An American tenor was making his debut in *Pagliacci* at La Scala Opera House in Milan. When he finished the exciting aria, "Vesta la Giubba" the audience applauded and Carbogno, an elderly man sitting down front, stood up and exclaimed, "Sing-a it again!"

The tenor, delighted by the request, did an encore. Carbogno, the opera lover, again leaped to his feet and implored, "Sing-a it again!"

After five encores the tenor walked to the edge of the stage and said, "Thank you, for your very gracious reception!"

Once more the old man shouted, "Sing-a it again!"

"I'm sorry, sir," begged the singer. "We must go on. I can't sing it again!"

"Yes!" declared the opera fan. "You sing-a it again, until-a you sing it right!"

"*Sing it again—until-a you sing it right!*"

A reporter approached Signora Zurlini backstage at the Chicago Opera House. "Tell me," he asked, "how do you manage to hold that high C for so long?"

"I hold it," said the soprano, "as long as the stage manager keeps sticking pins in my ass!"

*   *   *

Gaetano and Sandello, two old chess players, stopped their game in Central Park and commiserated with each other about the disadvantages of advancing age.

"Yeah," said Gaetano, "I now chase-a da girls only when it's-a downhill!"

*   *   *

On a construction job, Foster and O'Riley watched in amazement as Scortelli kept tapping himself upwards on the elbow.

"What the hell is he doing?" asked Foster.

"He's goosing himself," replied O'Riley.

"On the elbow?"

"Yeah," smiled the Irishman, "you know Italians don't know their ass from their elbow."

Pagoni, aged 88, wasn't feeling well and went to the doctor.

After an examination and some preliminary tests, the M.D. was baffled. "I'm going to have to take some more tests," said the physician. "Looks like you've got venereal disease or the measles."

Pagoni returned to the medic's office the following day. "I have bad news for you," said the doctor. "I'm afraid it's V.D.!"

"Of course," said the old Italian, "where would I come in-a contact with-a da measles?"

* * *

The voluptuous young secretary had just married Mapelli, her 86-year-old boss. They were spending their first evening at a hotel.

Mapelli came out of the bathroom, wearing a nightshirt and ready for action. He triumphantly extended his hand, all fingers spread.

"What!" shrieked his 22-year-old bride. "Five times?"

"No," said the old Italian, "just pick a finger!"

Farelli came from Itály, opened a restaurant, and became very successful. He still practiced the simplest form of bookkeeping—he kept the accounts payable in a cigar box, accounts due on a spindle, and cash in the register.

One day, his youngest son, who had just graduated as an economics major, said to him, "Pa, I don't see how you run your business this way. How do you know what your profits are?"

"Well, sonny boy," replied Farelli, "when I got off-a da boat I no have nothing but-a da pants I was-a wearing. Just-a da pants. Today you brother is a docta, you sister is-a da teach and you just-a graduate."

"I know, Papa, but..."

"You mama and me have a nice-a car, a nice-a house, a good-a buzyness, and everything is-a paid for. So you add all-a that together, you subtract-a da pants—and that's-a da profit."

* * *

Did you hear about the Italian businessman who went broke?

He imported 200,000 cans of underarm deodorant to Italy—and didn't sell a single one.

What is an Italian?
That's a Mexican with a job.

*　　*　　*

Telephone Operator: This is long distance from Chicago.

Tavoni in Boston: I know it's-a long-a distance from-a Chicago, so why you call-a me?

*　　*　　*

What do you get when you cross an Italian with a gorilla?

A moron who doesn't have to wear winter underwear.

*　　*　　*

What is Italian-matched crystal?

Three empty jars of the same brand of peanut butter.

*　　*　　*

What is smarter than a dumb Mexican?
A smart Italian.

At a Mafia party how can you tell the guest of honor?

He's the one with the brand new cement overcoat.

Did you hear about the Italian who was told by the mechanic that his car needed a new muffler?

He asked his wife to knit him one.

* * *

Tommy Lasorda, the lovable manager of the Los Angeles Dodgers, wins friends with this wacky whopper:

Three astronauts, a Russian, an American, and an Italian were discussing outer space. "There is no doubt in our minds," declared the Russian, "that we will be the first ones to land on Mars."

"No way," interrupted the American. "We've been on the moon fourteen times and *we're* going to be first on Mars."

"Well, you fellas canna fight all-a you want over landing on-a Mars," challenged the Italian. "We gonna be the first-a to land on the sun!"

"Don't be ridiculous!" said the American. "You can't land on the sun. It's too hot!"

"Aha, you think we a stupid or somethin'?" answered the Italian. "We know that! We gonna land at-a *night*!"

What is the most common way for Italians to commit suicide?

Gluttony.

*   *   *

A young social worker in Rome was visiting Mrs. Bacaloni, the mother of ten bambinos. The social worker realized her message was not getting across when the housewife commented:

"*Mia cara*, this-a birth control may be all-a right for you, but no for me. I'm-a married and I donna need it."

*   *   *

The whole Mafia is talking about the moll who walked out on her boyfriend when she found out he was just a finger man.

*   *   *

Did you hear about the Italian who made a fortune?

He bought 1,000 garbage trucks and then sold them to Polacks as condominiums with escalators.

Lou Wills, Jr., dancer/choreographer extraordinaire, also loves the laughs from this kind of looney levity:

Tony, the organ grinder, took his hand organ and monkey into a tavern to relax with a beer. He propped his organ against the bar, placed the monkey on the counter top and sat down beside Comstock, a bank-teller on his lunch break.

Promptly the ill-mannered monkey squatted on Comstock's martini, his genitals slopping into the cool liquid. The man quickly brushed the monkey away but the persistent primate strutted right back and sat squarely on top of his glass, his jangles again neatly mixing with the olive.

Now, Comstock became indignant and turned to the organ grinder. "Say," he grumbled, "do you know your monkey's got his balls in my drink?"

"No," replied Tony, "but if-a you hum a few bars I'll try an-a play it!"

"*You hum it—I play it!*"

Did you hear about the Italian gynecologist who set up a dual practice?

He delivered pizzas and babies at the same time.

*   *   *

Polchak, a Polish coal miner, was badly injured in an automobile crash and had to have a brain transplant. A team of surgeons put him under anesthesia, removed his brain, and went into the next room to get the new one.

When they returned to the operating room, Polchak was gone. The police searched everywhere for him but to no avail. He had vanished. The doctors contacted Interpol and they checked throughout the world trying to find this poor Pole who had left the hospital without his brain.

Finally, five years later, he was found. Polchak was teaching school in Italy.

*   *   *

Why are rectal thermometers banned in Italy?

They cause too much brain damage.

After two days in a coma, the patient woke up to find Dr. Cardoni standing beside his hospital bed.

"My friend, I got bad news for you," said the Sicilian sawbones. "I cut off your good leg by mistake. But I got good news, too. Your bad leg is getting well."

*   *   *

SIGN IN WINE FACTORY

Any Italian who wishes to attend the funeral of a relative must tell the foreman of his department on the day of the game

*   *   *

In recent years, American baseball has outlawed the so-called spitball. What do they call the same thing in Italian baseball?

A greaseball.

How did Panzini get to be the fastest runner in Italy?

His trainer told him that if he ever lost a race he'd have to take a bath.

* * *

Lucazzi: My brother ran a hundred yards in six seconds.

Bailey: But that's impossible! The world's record is more than nine seconds.

Lucazzi: My brother knows a shortcut.

* * *

Fitzgerald went to a bar for five consecutive nights and watched Manzini sitting over in a corner booth. It was an incredible sight. Good-looking, wildly shaped girls, alone or in groups of two or three, would wander in and soon make their way to the weird-looking Manzini.

"I don't understand it," grumbled Fitzgerald, to the bartender, "I don't see how the Eye-talian does it."

"Me, either!" said the barkeep. "I been watchin' him for weeks. He certainly ain't handsome, he's a lousy dresser, and he hardly never says a word. The guy just sits there licking his eyebrows!"

Carlo felt weak, tired, and rundown. He went to a doctor.

"I have sex with five, maybe six broads three times a day."

"Well," said the M.D., "that's the cause of your trouble."

"I'm glad to hear that, Doc," said the hot-blooded Italian. "I was afraid it might be the masturbation."

* * *

While dining at Recanti's Ristorante Falco found a hair in his spaghetti. He complained angrily to Recanti, the owner, and walked out.

About a week later, Recanti attended a Sons of Italy stag and recognized Falco up on stage going down on the belly dancer. After the performance, Recanti ran up to Falco and said, "You a big-a hypocrite. You complain about-a da hair in-a my spaghetti but here you eat-a this-a broad."

"Hell," said Falco, "if she had a piece-a spaghetti in her box, I wouldn't-a eat her either."

Zitto: Why you no wash-a you face? I can-a see what-a you had for breakfast this-a morning.

Delli: Okay, big-a shot-a. What I have?

Zitto: Pizza.

Delli: You wrong. That was-a yesterday.

* * *

A famous Italian movie producer living in Beverly Hills brought his mother over from Genoa to live with him. Mama immediately took over all the cooking chores.

One day she telephoned Jorgensen's, the posh grocery emporium, to give them an order. "I want a quart of a milk, a dozen eggs, a few apples, and an amatta!"

"I've got the milk, the eggs, and a few apples," said the clerk, checking the list, "but what's a matta?"

"Nothing's amatta wid me," replied the old woman. "What's amatta wid you?"

* * *

Ritano, hoping to get work at a steel mill, sat before the personnel manager.

"I was-a born in Italy!" said Ritano.

"What part?"

"All of me."

Did you hear about the Italian immigrant who thought "Established 1891" was the company's phone number?

* * *

Capozzi was digging ditches on one side of the street while 200 men worked on the other side. "How come you make-a me work on this side all-a time by myself?" asked the new arrival to America.

"You've got bad breath!" answered the foreman.

"Say, mista!" retorted the Italian. "If-a you kissed as many politicians as I did to get-a this-a job, you'd have-a bad breath-a too!"

* * *

Zitto: This is a very high-class suit I'm-a wearing. You never guess what I pay for it.

Delli: Ten dollars.

Zitto: Ah, that was just-a lucky guess.

Nigrelli was extolling the virtues of his newly adopted homeland. "This is a great-a country," he declared. "Look-a at Sinatra. Where else-a could a piece of spaghetti wind up-a with-a so mucha gravy!"

* * *

On a Third Avenue bus in Manhattan, a very prim spinster was shocked to hear the immigrant Olveri's conversation with his friend:

"Emma coma-a first, I come-a next, two ass-a come-a together. I come-a again, two ass-a come-a together again, I come-a once-a more, pee-pee twice, then I come-a for the last-a time."

When Olveri was finished, the crimson-faced old maid turned to a policeman sitting nearby.

"Aren't you going to arrest that terrible old man?" she whispered.

"Why?" asked the policeman. "For spelling 'Mississippi?'"

* * *

Did you hear about the Italian who flunked his citizenship test because he couldn't spell D.D.T.?

46

Pollini, a plumber's helper, had been sent out on a job. The lady of the house wasn't bad looking and in the course of the afternoon they heated up the bedroom pretty good.

About four o'clock the phone rang, and after answering the woman said to Pollini, "That was my husband. He'll be home soon but is leaving at seven-thirty. Why don't you come back this evening and we'll pick up where we left off!"

"What?" exclaimed the plumber. "On my own time?!"

*　*　*

Pasquale was being examined for naturalization as a U.S. citizen. "Who is the President of the United States?"

The foreigner answered correctly.

"And the Vice-President?"

Again he gave the right answer.

"Could you be President?"

"No! No!"

"Why not?"

"I'm-a too busy. I work-a in the barber shop all-a day now."

*　*　*

GENOVESE GREENHORNS

Giametti, newly arrived in New York from Genoa, walked into a Fifth Avenue bank.

" 'Scusa, please! I like-a to talk with-a the fella what arranges the loans."

"I'm sorry," said the guard, "but the loan arranger is out to lunch!"

"Okay," said the Italian, "then lemme talk-a to Tonto!"

Ramilli, newly arrived from the old country, entered a corner telephone booth and relieved himself.

When he came out, Ramilli reported to his cousin, "Hey, they gotta real-a nice outhouses in America. Lots-a paper and they even-a got-a telephone-a too!"

La Bella was being examined for citizenship. The first question the judge asked was, "How many states are there in the union?"

"I dunno," replied the immigrant. "I ask-a you how many banan' in a bunch. You dunno. You know-a you biz, I know-a mine."

* * *

D'Angelo had migrated to America and now he stood before the judge to find out whether he would get his citizenship papers.

"You Honor," said the frightened Italian, "I no speak-a too good-a Hingleesh 'cause I no be in this-a country too long-a time. Since-a I talk-a like thees, you think-a I'm-a no getta my papers?"

The judge said, "Donju worry, you gonna get-a you papers!"

* * *

Did you hear about the Italian who sat in a car wash one day for three hours because he thought it was raining too hard to drive?

Grandma Zottola, who had been voting in America for 30 years, finally decided to become a citizen. She arrived in court on the appointed day.

The first part of the test was on American History. The judge held up a picture of Abraham Lincoln and asked, "Who is this?"

"Dat's-a Abraham Linalink!" replied Mrs. Zottola.

His Honor then held up a picture of George Washington. "And who is this?" he inquired.

"Dats-a his wife!" answered Grandma with pride.

* * *

Zitto and Delli migrated from Italy and each Sunday they met at a New York park bench to while away the hours:

Zitto: This is-a some wonderful country. Where else could-a you walk down-a the street, meet a complete-a stranger, have-a dinner with him, and then he invite-a you to spend-a the night at-a his house?

Delli: This-a happen to you?

Zitto: To me, no—but it's-a happen to my sister.

Sambucci came over on a cattle boat from Italy. He worked for years, scrimping and saving to get the passage money. Finally he arrived in New York.

As he was getting off the boat he saw a deep-sea diver climbing out of the water onto the dock.

"How you like-a dis?" said the old man. "I spend-a money to take-a da boat and this-a guy he walk over!"

"How you like-a dat?
This-a guy he walk over!"

LETTER FROM NEWLY ARRIVED IMMIGRANT

Dear Mama,

They have a thing here to wash call-a da bathtub. I have-a da trouble first-a time I use it. A lota water she's-a come from out-a da faucets and she's-a keep-a runnin' down a hole in-a da bottom. But I soon-a figure it out and everything is-a now okay. I just-a sit on-a da hole and wash-a at the same-a time.

You lovin' son,
Umberto

*   *   *

Did you hear about the Italian immigrant who ran off the bus backwards because he heard a woman passenger say she was going to pinch his seat when he got off?

*   *   *

Handyman Zuccheri was painting the library in a wealthy banker's home. He spotted a moosehead on the wall.

"Atsa nice moose," said the Italian.

"Thank you," said the banker.

"You mind if I go in-a da next room to see the rest of it?"

Did you hear about Manzini the brick-layer?

He went crazy trying to lay a cornerstone in a roundhouse.

* * *

Two laborers, Pacetti and Deloro, were working at a project.

"Hey," shouted Pacetti, "stop throwin' that dirt out-a da ditch!"

"But," said Deloro, "I'm-a diggin'-a da ditch and I gotta throw the dirt-a somewhere."

"Well," said the first Italian, "dig another hole-a and put it there."

* * *

Construction Worker:	I hear the men are striking.
Bartocci:	What-a for?
Construction Worker:	Shorter hours.
Bartocci:	Good for them. I always did think-a sixty minutes was-a too long for an hour.

Rancati and Zuccato were out in a row boat fishing. Suddenly Rancati landed a big one. "Wow!" said Rancati. "This is-a some place to fish. How we gonna remember it?"

Zuccato immediately leaped over board and disappeared beneath the surface.

In a moment he climbed back on board. "What-a you did?" asked Rancati.

"So we can remember this-a spot," answered Zuccato, "I paint-a the X on-a da bottom of-a the boat!"

"You must-a be stupid or something!" shouted Rancati. "What-a we gonna do if next time we no get-a da same boat!"

* * *

Salvatorelli arrived in America and in a short while his relatives taught him to say "apple pie and coffee" in English so he could order in a restaurant. The next day the immigrant walked into a coffee shop. "What would you like?" asked the waitress. "Apple-a pie and-a coffee." replied Salvatorelli.

Since that was all he could say he was forced to eat apple pie and coffee every day for a week. When he complained to his cousins they taught him to say "ham sandwich."

Armed with the new addition to his vocabulary Salvatorelli said to the waitress, "Ham sandwich."

"White or rye?" asked the girl.

"Apple-a pie and-a coffee." said the Italian.

*   *   *

Giuseppi wanted to write a letter to his wife back in Palermo. He said to his son, "Joe, tell-a me something, please."

"What is it, Pop?"

"How you spell sence?"

"S-e-n-s-e."

"Naa, sence-a, sence. How you spell-a sence?"

"C-e-n-t-s," said his son.

"Naa, naa!"

"That's the only way I know. S-e-n-s-e or c-e-n-t-s."

"Naa, looka Joe, I'm write your mama in Asbury Park and I wanna tell her nobody's-a wash the dishes sence-a last Thursday."

Gene Gach, humor-loving director of California Orphanage Vista Del Mar, tells this tempting tidbit of tomfoolery:

One summer in New York a gorilla had escaped from a traveling circus. As Bronzini was walking down Broadway, the ape suddenly appeared and sidled up beside the Italian.

An astonished police officer directing traffic rushed over to the unusual sight of Bronzini and the gorilla.

"Hey," said the cop, "what are you doing with that ape?"

"I don't know," said Bronzini. "He just-a come up and-a take-a walk-a with me!"

"You better take that ape to the zoo!"

"Okay, boss!" said the Italian.

The next day the same policeman spotted Bronzini and the gorilla walking hand in hand along Park Avenue. The cop was livid. "Just a minute," he shouted to Bronzini. "I told you yesterday to take that ape to the zoo!"

"I did," said the Italian, "and he like-a it so much, today I'm-a take-a him to the movin' picture show!"

"Hallo, TWA Airlines?" said Vecchi over the phone. "How long-a it takes to fly-a to Roma?"

"Just a minute," said the reservations clerk.

"Thank-a you so much!" said Vecchi and hung up.

* * *

Oldoni, the immigrant, had to travel by train from New York to Raleigh, North Carolina. When he was met by a cousin, it was obvious that Oldoni was in a very bad mood.

"What happened?" asked his relative.

"Ah, that goddamn-a conductor he tell-a me no do this and no do that!" exclaimed the Italian. "I take out-a my sand-a-wich and he say, 'No—in-a dining car.' I start-a drink-a some vino and he say, 'No—in-a club-a car.' So I go in-a club-a car, meet a girl, and she take-a me back to her empty compartment and then the goddamn conductor he come along-a yellin', 'No 'foka, Virginia, No-foka, Virginia!"

Ten years after his arrival in America, Roselli had saved enough money from his fruit and vegetable business to build a huge house.

"I wanna three bedrooms-a upstairs," he explained to the builder. "I wanna large-a living room with a nice-a big-a staircase leading up to the bedroom. And right over here next to the staircase I wanna hollow statue."

Months later he returned and found everything built to his specifications. Then he noticed a statue next to the staircase.

"Hey, what's-a matta wid you?" shouted Roselli. "You no capish what I tell-a you!"

"Isn't that what you ordered?" asked the builder, "A hollow statue?"

"Are you-a stupid or something?" cried the Italian. "I wanna one-a those things that goes a ring-a ring. you pick 'em up and say 'hallo, is tat choo?' "

"*I wanna da ting dat does a ring-a-ring and you say 'Hallo is tat choo?'*"

Zitto: My daughter Josephina, she's-a spend all-a her time with Socrates, Aristotle, and a Plato.

Delli: What's-a matta, she no like-a da American boys?

* * *

As an experiment, two scientists decided to mate a human male with a female gorilla. They agreed only someone really dumb would submit to such an act. So they went down to the docks and grabbed Panelli, who had just gotten off the boat.

"We'll give you five thousand dollars to go to bed with a gorilla!" proposed one of the scientists. "Will you do it?"

"Okay. I do it!" agreed the immigrant. "But on three conditions!"

"What are they?" asked the men of science.

"First-a, I'm-a only gonna do it-a once!" said the Italian. "Second-a, nobody can-a watch. And a third-a, if a baby is a born, it's-a gotta be raised a Catholic!"

Calzoni was being given a test to see if he qualified to become a U.S. citizen. The examiner was trying to explain allegiance to the flag. Calzoni did not understand.

Finally the examiner asked, "Do you know what flies over the courthouse?"

"Sure, boss," said the Italian, "peedgins."

* * *

Zitto: How can-a you be so stupid?
Delli: Well, it ain't-a something you can-a pick up over-a night.

* * *

Did you hear about the Italian who thought bacteria was the rear entrance to a café?

Luchessi arrived in the United States and within a few weeks felt the great need to have a woman. He tried flirting with a few at a nearby bar but was unsuccessful because he spoke very little English.

Finally, one night he picked up a street walker and she took him to his apartment. They were in bed making violent love when suddenly Luchessi realized that he hadn't spoken a single word to her.

"Miss-a," he said, "I come-a from-a da other side!"

"Oh?" said the girl. "This I gotta see!"

*　　*　　*

SEXY SICILIANS

Miss Ticconi, a new Al Italia stewardess, was summoned to the office of the head of the airline's training program.

"I've been-a told about that episode on you first flight," said the female supervisor. "From now on when a male-a passenger feels-a faint, I'll expect you to push his head down between *his own* legs!"

* * *

"Hey, Paul, I just found out my new secretary, Miss Sandelli, is ambidexterous."

"What do you mean?"

"She takes dictation on both her knees."

Sandra, the sexy Hollywood starlet, checked into a Rome Hotel with a famous Italian movie producer.

"Mr. Paliglia, be honest now," she asked. "Do I have a chance of becoming a big star?"

"Honey," said Taliglia, glancing downward, "you already making it-a big!"

* * *

Candulla entered a crowded subway with his six children. Only six seats were vacant and each of the kids ran to a seat. The Italian was left standing.

"Hey," chuckled a nearby passenger, "it looks like you've screwed yourself out of a seat!"

* * *

Shoe Salesman: Can I interest you in a casual pump?
Miss Passoni: Sure! I can look at shoes later.

* * *

While visiting a small African country, a Frenchman, a Norwegian, and an Italian were found guilty of raping a native woman. Since the crime was a sexual offense, the penalty would also be sexual. Each man was condemned to lose his penis.

They were brought before the emperor and then given a choice of how the penalty would be carried out.

The Frenchman, who had grown up in the land of the guillotine, cried, "Chop it off!"

The Norwegian had known only the bitter cold so he shouted, "Freeze it off!"

The Emperor then asked the Italian, "And how about you?"

"I'm ready," answered the sex-mad Italian. "Jerk it off!"

*　　*　　*

Dominic was an inexperienced lover. He was in bed with a sexy doll but, unfortunately, wasn't giving her what she wanted.

"I'm sorry," he apologized, "I'm all thumbs tonight!"

"I knew you were using the wrong finger!" she snapped.

OLD SICILIAN SAYING

*When in Rome do as the Romans do
—pinch some broad on the ass!*

* * *

Sarvito, Mennini, and Doronzo, three Sardinian sheep ranchers, were hurt in a plane crash while on a hunting trip in Africa. They were sent to recuperate in a Moroccan hospital. In Morocco, they allow the shepherds to bring their flocks into town to eat the grass, which also helps keep the blades short.

One day, the Italians, confined to their hospital room for several months, looked out a window and saw a herd of sheep enjoying a grass lunch. Sarvito pointed to a plump ewe and exclaimed, "I wish-a that one was-a Sophia Loren."

"I wish-a that was-a Racquel-a Welch,"

"I just-a wish it was-a dark," said Doronzo.

* * *

Did you hear about the Italian teenager who explained to his doctor that he had contracted VD during a wet dream?

Poor Pete was known as "Broomstick" among his friends. He was awfully skinny and looked so emaciated it did not help his social life. One night, to drown his sorrow, Pete wandered into a bar in New York's Little Italy and by some miracle became friendly with Rosalie, a buxom divorcee. He nearly fainted when she invited him home.

At her apartment, she lead Mr. Skin-and-Bones directly to the bedroom and said, "Why don't you get undressed and wait for me in bed?"

Pete ripped off his clothes and, panting with excitement, waited for her return.

Five minutes later, the Italian girl walked in with a six-year-old boy. She threw back the bedsheets, pointed to Pete and exclaimed, "Now, you see, Roberto, that's what you're gonna look like if you don't start eating your spaghetti!"

*　　*　　*

"Doc, I gotta see you," said Guidini on the telephone. "I think I got gonorrhea!"

"Okay, but first you've got to make a date with my nurse."

"I did, Doc. That's why I gotta see ya!"

71

Cleopatra (to her Roman love) :
   "You're an easy Mark, Antony . . ."

* * *

The teacher asked the question, "What is the most beautiful thing in the world?"

"Flowers," answered one little girl.

"The sunset," offered another youngster.

Nunzio raised his hand and said, "Bein' pregnant!"

"What?" exploded the teacher.

"Well, my big sister came home last night and said, 'Pop, I'm pregnant.' And my father said, 'Well, that's beautiful! Just beautiful!' "

* * *

Did you hear about the Italian girl who had to make up her mind between her two boyfriends?

They couldn't get on together!

After lights-out at an exclusive girls' school, the conversation turned to the best method of avoiding pregnancy.

"My boyfriend pulls out before he comes off," said a Jewish girl, "but I know that's not very safe, so I'm going to get some pills during the holidays."

"I've been using the rhythm method," said an Irish girl, "but that means I can't have it very often. I think I'll go on the pill, too."

"I wouldn't advise it," said an Italian girl, "I've tried and it keeps dropping out."

* * *

Capelli was visiting Paris for the first time.

"*Monsieur*," the French guide announced to his Italian client, "we are now passing the most fabulous brothel in all of France."

"Why?" asked the Italian.

Garrity's member was 25 inches long. The poor man couldn't find a woman who could hold him. The doctors couldn't help, so he went to a little side-street sex shop.

The clerk showed Garrity a stick of peppermint candy and said, "This has a secret medication inside. As you suck, your stump shortens. In your case, about five minutes ought to do the trick. But let me warn you, the drug makes you very sleepy and drowsy, so you must have someone there to pull it out of your mouth when the time's up."

Garrity couldn't wait to try the miraculous treatment. He dashed into the nearest men's room, handed the Italian attendant twenty bucks and said, "I'm popping a medicated rod in my mouth, and it might make me doze off. It's extremely important that you pull out the dopestick after five minutes."

Garrity woke up several hours later, saw the attendant watching him, and asked, "Did you remove the stick after five minutes?"

The man replied, "No spikka da English."

Natalia was washing her hair in the bathroom when her roommate called out, "Natie, you have an obscene phone call!"

"Get his number," replied the Italian girl. "I'll call him back!"

* * *

The telephone rang and Rick picked it up. "Hello," said the voice, "this is Vinnie. Come on over, I'm having a wild party."

"Gee, I'd love to," said Rick, "but I got a bad case of gonorrhea."

"Bring it along," said Vinnie, "the way things are going, my friends'll drink anything!"

* * *

Did you hear about the Italian girl who swallowed a pin when she was a child, but didn't feel a prick until she was sixteen?

* * *

What did the Italian say when his sister had a baby?

"I'll be a monkey's uncle!"

"Hey, Enzo, how'd your sister Angie get that black eye?"

"She was jumping rope and forgot to put on her bra!"

Tebaldi and his wife were in a movie theater. When they got up to leave, the woman suddenly exclaimed, "Hey, my ass is-a fall asleep!"

"You *stupido*!" said Vic. "I heard of an arm or a leg-a fallin' asleep, but I no hear of-a da ass."

Just then the man sitting behind them said, "She's absolutely right, mister! Her ass did fall asleep. In fact, I heard it snoring!"

* * *

Did you hear about the very wealthy Italian hostess on Park Avenue?

She wears mink all day and fox all night.

* * *

Mrs. Paglia saw a store display of seductive nightgowns. "What's them?" she asked.

"They're sexy lingerie," explained the clerk. "You wear them to bed to get some action started. Would you like to buy one?"

"Atsa no help," said the country woman. "When-a my husband and me hit-a da sheets every night, we both-a too tired to do anything except-a screw and sleep."

The john had finished with Miss Frucci, and after paying her said, "You ever been picked up by the fuzz?"

"Sure I have," said the Italian hooker, "and it hurts like hell!"

* * *

Salvadore had lived in the Italian hills so long that when he slept with his first girl he didn't know what to do. She tried to help, but he just didn't understand about coupling. Finally she sighed and said, "Take the hardest thing you've got and put it where I make pee-pee."

So he got his boccie ball and dropped it in the sink.

* * *

Gino went to an optometrist and asked for a new pair of glasses.

"But you just got a new pair last week."

"I know," said Gino, "but I got them-a broken in an accident."

"How?" asked the optometrist.

"I was kissin' my girl," said the Italian.

"How the hell could you break your glasses kissing a girl?"

"She crossed her legs."

Aspiring Denver actor Larry Sanchez tells about the night Mrs. Mantoni got into a taxi. After riding awhile she realized she'd forgotten her pocketbook and had no money to pay the fare. The meter now read $7.

"Mista Driver," she cried. "You betta stop. I no can-a pay you!"

"Oh, that's all right," said the cabbie. "I'll just pull down a dark street, get in the back seat with you, take off your panties . . ."

"Mista, you gonna got gypped," said the Italian lady. "My panties only cost-a eighty-nine cents!"

"My panties only cost-a
eighty-nine cents!"

Pinkie, just out of the Big House, was met by his old buddy, Louie. As they drove away from the prison, Pinkie said, "I got-a have a broad quick. What happened to that sexy stripper with the big boobs that worked down at Rick's Club?"

"Dincha know?" said Louie. "She died."

"Gee, that's too bad. What she die from?"

"Gonorrhea."

"Hey, c'mon. Nobody dies from gonorrhea."

"You do, if you give it to Big Eddie."

*　*　*

Did you hear about the Italian girl who saw a sign in the post office: PROSTITUTE WANTED?

She went in and applied for the job.

*　*　*

John Francis, Hollywood's premier concert show producer, provided this pinch of persiflage:

Corporal Torlonia had been overseas for 18 months. He came home and found he had a three-week-old baby. His wife explained that she dreamt she had intercourse with him, and she got pregnant.

Torlonia sued for divorce. In court even the judge was astounded by the wife's story. He stood up and asked the audience if they ever had intercourse with a ghost.

In the back, Torlonia's father raised his hand. His honor called him to the bench.

"Now," said the judge, "you say you had intercourse with a ghost?"

"Oh, 'scusa," said the elderly Italian. "I thought-a you say-a goat!"

*   *   *

Did you hear about the Italian girl who wanted to be a gangster's moll but a finger man got her in the end?

*   *   *

DiSapio and Nittola were watching a solidly built woman waddling down Mulberry Street in New York's Little Italy.

"Hey," said DiSapio, "that's a nice pizza ass."

Al Vargos, Montebello's celebrated catering Casanova, came up with this crackerjack:

A gorilla in the zoo died. His female companion, after a few months, began getting violent as her need for sex increased. The zookeepers decided to get a man to make love to her. They picked up Balgani down on skidrow, and offered him $20 for the job.

They muzzled the she-ape, tied her arms to the bars, and let Balgani gingerly into her cage. When the gorilla saw that Balgani had an erection, she suddenly ripped her arms loose from the bars and began crushing him in her embrace. "Help!" he shouted, "for God's sake, help!"

"Don't worry," the keepers shouted back, "we'll get an elephant-gun and shoot her."

"No! No! Don't shoot her. Just get her muzzle off—I wanna kiss her!"

"Don't shoot! I wanna kiss her!"

The three Gagliardi girls were all married on the same day, and that night their parents listened at the bedroom doors. They heard the first daughter laughing and the second crying and the third silent. The next morning their mother took them aside and asked them to explain.

"Well," said the first, "you always told me to laugh when something tickled me."

"Mama," said the second, "you always told me to cry when something hurt me."

"Well," said the third, "you always told me not to speak when I had my mouth full."

*　　*　　*

Benson returned to Naples, where, as a youngster during the war, he had befriended a native named Capitini. When the Italian saw Benson, he simply couldn't do enough for him, and insisted that he meet his sister.

"Is she pretty?" asked Benson.

"Ah! Bella! Bella!" cried Capitini.

"Is she young?" continued Benson.

"Si! Si!"

"And, is she pure?" asked Benson.

The Italian shrugged and exclaimed, "You Americans are all crazy."

On a road ten miles from Palermo, Lawson, an American motorist, was stopped by a masked desperado who, brandishing a revolver, demanded in a thick Sicilian accent that he get out of the automobile.

Lawson obeyed. "Take my money, my car," he pleaded, "but don't kill me!"

"I no kill-a you," replied the Italian, "if you do what I say." Whereupon, he told Lawson to unzip his pants and masturbate. Though shocked, the American did what he was told.

"Good," said the masked stranger. "Now-a do it again." Lawson protested, but the gun was pointed at his head, so with extreme difficulty, he repeated the act.

"Again," commanded the desperado, "or I kill-a you!" Summoning superhuman resources, the exhausted motorist relieved himself yet a third time.

The Italian gave an order and a beautiful young girl stepped out from behind the rocks. "Now," said the highwayman, "you can give-a my sister a ride into town!"

* * *

DOLCE DEFINITIONS

ABALONE—*An expression of disbelief*

* * *

AH FONG GOO—*Chinese-Italian restaurant*

* * *

BIGAMIST—*Severe fog in Naples*

* * *

BIGOTRY—*An Italian redwood*

COLUMBUS DAY—*The Italian Yom Kippur*

*   *   *

COPULATE—*What an Italian police chief says to an officer who doesn't get to work on time*

*   *   *

FORMAL ITALIAN DINNER—*When all the men come to the table with their flies zipped up*

*   *   *

FUNDSALOW—*Poor Italian's plight*

*   *   *

INNUENDO—*An Italian suppository*

*   *   *

ITALIAN DIAPHRAGM—*A Wop stopper*

ITALIAN GIRDLE—*A venetian bind*

*   *   *

ITALIAN SLUM—*Spaghetto*

*   *   *

THE ITALIAN
SUMMERTIME SONG—*Summa Time
I'm Happy,
Summa Time
I'm . . .*

*   *   *

OPERA—*Italian vaudeville*

*   *   *

OPERETTA—*A girl who works for the
phone company*

*   *   *

PIZZA—*A broiled manhole cover*

*   *   *

SPECIMEN—*An Italian astronaut*

SORRENTO STUD—*An Italian who rips off a girl's brassiere and then bites her on the ear*

*   *   *

TITERIA—*A brassiere factory in Italy*

*   *   *

VICE VERSA—*Dirty poetry from Italy*

*   *   *

MUSSOLINI'S MOUSEKETEERS

What was the name of Mussolini's flagship?

"Chicken of the Sea."

*　　*　　*

One day, Mussolini, at the height of his power, slipped unnoticed into a movie theatre. When the newsreels came on and his own image appeared on the screen, everyone, except the Italian dictator rose and cheered. The man next to Mussolini tapped him on the shoulder and said, "You betta stand up-a. We all feel-a da way you do, but it's-a no safe to show it."

Why did Mussolini have six bullets in him when he was found dead?

Because 200 Italian sharpshooters were firing at him.

* * *

Why was the Italian navy so useless during the war?

The cannons were too heavy and all three garbage scows sank.

* * *

What's the easiest way to spot an Italian ship?

When it's put on water—it sinks.

* * *

Why did the Italian navy disband their underwater demolition team?

They kept leaving an oil slick.

* * *

How do you sink an Italian submarine?
Put it in water.

How did Mussolini review his fleet?
Through a glass-bottomed boat.

* * *

NEWS FLASH
*The Italian navy has just turned several
hundred lighthouses upside down to
guide their submarines home*

* * *

Why do so many Italian submarines sink?
Because of the screen doors in the hull.

* * *

How do they separate the men from the boys in the Italian navy?
With a crowbar.

* * *

WORLD WAR TWO JINGLE
*Whistle while you work
Hitler likes to jerk
Mussolini broke his weenie
Now it doesn't work*

Rudy Deluca, the talented television and motion picture screenwriter, tells this titilator:

Merani and Servano, two sailors aboard an Italian freighter, were torpedoed during World War II. They managed to save themselves by clinging to a life raft.

Suddenly, Merani noticed a periscope skimming the water. He nudged his comrade and said, "Hey, is that a U-boat?"

"No!" said Servano seeing the periscope. "Atsa no my boat!"

"Atsa no my boat!"

American ships have "U.S.S." in front of their names. It means: United States Ship.

British ships are preceeded by "H.M.S.," which means: Her Majesty's Ship.

Italian ships during World War II were ordered by Mussolini to be prefaced by the letters "A.M.B": Atsa My Boat.

*　*　*

What's the only thing smaller than the Swiss navy?

The Italian air force.

*　*　*

What would be a good description of 250 Italian paratroopers?

Air pollution.

*　*　*

Why was the Italian air force so quickly defeated at the outbreak of World War II?

They didn't have enough rubber bands to work the propellers of their planes.

Scarmella was a flyer during World War II. He'd never shot down a British plane and everybody in the squadron kidded him about it.

One day while on patrol Scarmella spotted five British transport planes. He zipped into their formation and shot down all five.

Now he couldn't wait to tell his fellow pilots. Scarmella landed quickly, jumped out of his plane and rushed over to a colonel standing beside a map table.

"I just-a shoot-a down five-a British-a transports!" shouted the proud Italian.

"I say, bad luck, old chap!" replied the officer.

* * *

FOR SALE

10,000 genuine Italian army rifles. Cheap. Have never been fired. Have been used only once.

* * *

Did you hear about the Italian tanks? They're the only ones with back-up lights.

Did you hear about the five-speed Italian tank used in World War II?

It had four gears in reverse and one speed forward—in case the enemy got behind them.

*   *   *

SOCIETY PAGE ITEM

Members of the Italian Suicide Squad will meet next week for their 35th Anniversary Reunion

*   *   *

During World War II, Hermann Goebbels rushed into Hitler's office and said, "We are having trouble with our sewage disposal. We need to have a larger processing plant."

"We can have the largest sewage processing plant in the world!" exclaimed the Führer.

"How?" asked Goebbels.

"Just build a levy around Italy!" replied the German dictator.

What is the first tactical training given to Italian army recruits?
How to retreat.

* * *

When the Italians went to war, the first requisition the quartermaster received was for two million white handkerchiefs.

* * *

Grizzled veterans of the Afrika Korps who fought with Italian troops during the desert campaigns remember that the Italian's favorite song was "I Surrender Dear."

* * *

How do you train Italians to be soldiers?
First teach them to raise their hands above their heads.

* * *

What do you call a Neopolitan with a war medal?
A thief.

Roy Battocchio, RCA Record's dynamic artists-relations manager, regales pals with this rib-buster:

Sergeant Lampazzi told Private Roccatano to go to the end of the line. He did but then returned. "I thought I tol-a you go to the end of the line," barked the NCO. "Why you come-a back?"

"Because," explained the private, "There's-a somebody there already!"

"There's-a somebody already there!"

Toward the end of World War II when the Italians were fighting the Germans, the Nazi soldiers came up with a scheme to kill many of Mussolini's men.

They simply yelled, "Hey, Luigi!" When an Italian infantryman stuck his head up and answered, "*Si?*" boom! He was dead.

That's all the Krauts did: "Luigi?" "*Si?*" Boom!

After thousands of Italians had been wiped out they decided to retaliate. They figured that every German's name was Hans. So an Italian captain shouted, "Hey, Hans!"

Silence. "Hey, Hans!" he repeated.

"Is that you Luigi?"

"*Si!*"

Boom!

* * *

It is not a very well-known fact that a poor peasant named Paoli was awarded Italy's highest honor for saving two women during the war.

One for himself and one for the general.

In the Middle East, during the Six Day War, the Israelis attacked the Arabs and two hours later the Italian army surrendered.

* * *

Just after Mussolini took over as dictator, he is reputed to have made this proclamation:

"What-a I want-a in dis-a country is-a less-a whoopie and more-a wopie!"

* * *

Just as World War II was ending, the Italian partisan snuck up and killed the last German soldier left in his village.

Then he yelled to his mother nearby, "Look, Mama, no Hans!"

* * *

What is the thinnest book in the world? *The History of Italian War Heroes.*

Super Studley, Hollywood's top celebrity photographer, breaks up buddies with this beaut:

A German, a Frenchman, and an Italian were captured during World War II and brought to a prison camp. "How many pairs of underwear do you need?" asked the quartermaster sergeant.

"Seven!" said the German. "A pair for each day of the week!"

"Four!" said the Frenchman. "One for each week in the month!"

"And what about you, Luigi?" asked the sergeant. "How many pairs of underwear do you need?"

"Twelve!" replied the Italian.

"What the hell do you need twelve for?"

"One-a for January, one-a for February, one-a . . ."

*   *   *

NAUGHTY NEAPOLITANS

"Hey, Dante, where'd you get the black eye?"

"Aw, I was over at my girl's house," explained the young stud, "and we was dancin' together real tight when her father walked in!"

"So?"

"So," said the Italian, "the old guy's deaf. He couldn't hear the music!"

* * *

"Hey, Sal, how'd your sister Rina make out on her driver's license test?"

"She flunked. When the car stalled, from force of habit, she jumped into the back seat."

Baffoni went to the doctor. "There's nothing really wrong with you," said the M.D. after an examination. "You're just sexually frustrated. Go out tonight, find yourself a woman, and have a good time."

That night Baffoni picked up a lady of the evening and spent a pleasurable hour with her.

After she dressed the girl said, "That'll be thirty bucks!"

"What?" said Baffoni. "You no unnerstan'. I do this on-a orders from-a the doctor."

"That's fine," said the prostie, "but I gotta get paid."

"Okay," said the Italian, "but you got-a wait for da Blue Cross!"

* * *

Miss Gambioni was a new patient and quite pretty. The doctor took her name and background and then said, "In order to determine what's wrong with you. I'll have to give you a thorough examination. Please get completely undressed."

"Okay, Doc," said the Italian beauty, "but to make me feel right, *you first!*"

Did you hear about the Italian girl who almost ruined her health by going to the doctor?

She thought he prescribed three hearty males a day.

* * *

Elena Diamond, the beautiful Los Angeles bank exec, stepped into an exclusive lingerie shop and inquired about a particular bra. Miss Tetrazini, behind the counter, told her, "We got them in cup sizes, A, B, C, D, and M."

"Size M?" queried Elena, "What's that?"

The Italian girl shook her hand from the wrist and answered, *"Ma-rone!"*

* * *

Cookie: Isn't your new boyfriend Eye-talian?
Cassie: Yeah, and does he think a lot of himself. He's so conceited he put a mirror on his bathroom ceiling so he could watch himself gargle.

Lofredo showed up at his date's house wearing a shirt that had water dripping from it.

"What's going on?" asked his girlfriend. "Why is your shirt soaking wet?"

"Well," said the Italian, "it said on the label 'Wash and Wear!'"

* * *

Martin Leeds, the brilliant Beverly Hills legal beagle, loves this lighthearted lulu:

"Miss Zattoli, you claim this is the man that stole the hundred-dollar bill you had pinned inside your brassiere?" asked the judge.

"Yes, your honor," she replied. "That's him!"

"Why didn't you put up a fight?" asked the jurist. "How come you didn't scream or kick? You certainly could've scratched him."

"Your honor, I would have," said the Italian girl, "but at that time I didn't know he was after my money!"

Louisa, the fourteen-year-old Salvatelli girl, developed a real nice figure, and she began to take a strong interest in the neighborhood studs. "I'm getting worried about Louisa," said Mrs. Salvatelli. "She spends too much time in the churchyard with the boys."

"Girls will be girls," said the old man, "You did it at her age."

"Yeah, but I didn't come home with my panties starched and-a ten dollars worth of quarters."

"Is that all? It could-a be worse."

"It is. Yesterday I found 'In Loving Memory' imprinted on the back of her best school coat."

* * *

Annalisa and Roberta, two Rome hotel chambermaids, were talking when the bell rang, and Annalisa had to go up to the room of an American tourist. He pushed her down on the bed, took his will, and in less than five minutes she was back downstairs.

"What did he want?" asked Roberta.

"I dunno. I think he must-a forgot himself."

Vito's mother shouted to him, "What-a you doin' up-a there?"

"I'm up here fingering my guitar," said Vito.

"Well, you better wash-a you hands good before you come-a down-a for supper."

* * *

Did you hear about the Italian who lost his job at the local massage parlor because he rubbed a female customer the wrong way?

* * *

Helen, a Polish girl, wanted to marry Frank, an Italian boy. But Helen's mother absolutely refused to allow the match.

"Sorry, Frank," said the girl, "but my mother thinks you're too feminine!"

"That's all right," said the Italian, "compared to her, I probably am!"

Silvana, who came from a small town in Italy, took a cruise in the hope of meeting an eligible bachelor.

As the ship rounded the coast of Africa it hit a storm, the girl was tossed overboard and washed up on the beach.

"Ah!" said the cannibal who found her, "I'm going to eat you!"

"Does that mean we're engaged?" asked the Italian girl.

* * *

"Did you hear what Rosella's friends did for her before her marriage?"

"No."

"Instead of giving her a shower, they made her take one."

* * *

Two Brooklyn stenos were having lunch:

Miss Oficci: I'm so nervous I forgot to take the pill yesterday.

Miss Ignoto: That's okay. You know what I do with my birth control pills? I feed them to storks.

Morris Resner, the Slavenburg Corporation's top exec, reminisces over this bit of ribaldry:

In pre-refrigerator days, the iceman was the butt of many a joke. He was the town "lay" and couldn't be trusted further than one could throw an icebox. The stories usually went something like this.

A comely housewife found that her clock had stopped. She went to the window, saw the ice wagon, and yelled down, "Hey, Piero! You gotta da time?"

"Sure," shouted Piero, "soon as I can find-a somebody to hold-a my horse!"

"*I find-a somebody to hold-a my horse!*"

In the days of the Roman Empire, many Italian men thought that sex was a pain in the ass. Of course, that was before Vaseline was discovered.

* * *

"Why are there so many homosexuals in Italy?"

"If you grew up around so many ugly broads, what else would you want to be?"

* * *

A motorcycle cop stopped Armando on the highway. He leered at the police officer and pursed his lips, grinning from ear to ear.

"Wipe that smile off your face, fella!" said the policeman to the faggot.

"What," lisped Armando, "and ruin my make-up?"

* * *

Did you hear about the two fairies in Naples who had a misunderstanding?

They went outside and exchanged blows.

"I like to eat, drink, and be Mary," said Fasalino, the fairy.

*   *   *

"Hey, Palucci, how come-a I no see you 'round no more?"

"I gotta new business now but I'm-a no do so good."

"What's-a you bus-y-ness?"

"I'm a pump."

"What-a the hell is a pump?"

"I gotta these eight girls who work-a for me, and everytime they go out and make-a fun with a guy, I make-a money."

"You be-a dope. You ain't-a da pump. You-a pimp!"

"No wonder business is no so good. In the *Yellow Pages*, I'm-a listed under 'Pump!'"

*   *   *

Did you hear about the gypsy girl who had to give up wearing garlic around her neck?

It kept the vampires away all right, but it attracted too many Italians.

Gannon, staying in a small Rome hotel, called the desk and said, "Send me up a whore!"

Mrs. Agostini, the owner's wife, was shocked and demanded that her husband throw the man out. But he was afraid, so Mrs. Agostini decided to go up and throw him out herself.

In a few moments, the husband could hear the sound of furniture breaking, and screams and curses.

Finally, Gannon came downstairs panting, his face scratched and his shirt torn. As he walked out he confided to Agostini, "That was a tough old bitch you sent up, but I screwed her anyway!"

* * *

Linelli said to his daughter, "I no like-a that Irish boy takin'-a you out. He's-a rough and common. And besides, he's a big-a dumbell."

"No, Papa!" replied the girl. "Tim's the most clever fella I know."

"Why you say that?"

"We've only been dating nine weeks and already he's cured me of that little illness I used to get every month."

Lovable Sidney Miller, the well-known Hollywood actor, writer, and director, knocked off these lusty limericks especially for this edition:

This Love Story's well worth repeating.
A Mafia guy sent a greeting
  Which, on Valentine's Day,
  Took his girl's breath away
'Cause the heart he sent her was still beating.

My lovely Maria was strong
For years she and I got along.
  She'd always surrender
  To music, so tender—
And she'd do it to me for a song!

* * *

Flanagan was sitting in a saloon and asked Gabrizzi for a light.

"I'm a no smoke," said the Italian, "but I gotta match somewhere." He emptied out all his pockets and produced six packets of aspirins and a four boxes of cough drops.

"What's the matter," asked the Irishman, "you got flu or something?"

"No," said Gabrizzi, "every time I go to the drug store. they only got women behind the counter."

119

Dino was making pretty good time with Sally, the office steno. She agreed to go away for the weekend, provided he brought a sheath with him.

When they went upstairs to bed, he admitted he didn't know how to wear it, so she rolled it down his thumb to show him. Then they put out the light and really went at it.

In a few minutes Sally said, "I'm really sticky, I think you broke that thing."

"No, I ain't," said Dino switching on the light, "here it is, still on my thumb."

*   *   *

Emilio and Tommaso, two young farmers, were mowing hay when they spotted two female cyclists from the city, picnicking in the grass. The boys told them they'd have to pay for flattening the hay, but the liberated ladies suggested paying on their backs. Emilio and Tommaso agreed and the girls produced condoms, saying, "You've got to wear these to prevent disease."

Two weeks later Tommaso said, "Hey, Emilio, you gotta disease?"

"No," answered his friend.

"Me, neither. Let's take-a these damn things off."

* * *

A family wedding took place in a small town outside Napoli. The house was crowded with people, and at bedtime everybody had to "double up." Marcella, the 16-year-old bridesmaid, who had come over from New York for the occasion, was put to bed with cousin Claudio, a year older.

After fidgeting around, the girl said, "Let's change sides, you roll over me, and I'll roll over you."

"Atsa okay," said the lad, "I just-a get out and walk around."

This happened several more times and the frustrated Marcella said, "Hey, I don't think you really understand what I want!"

"Oh, yes, I do," he said, "you wanna the whole damn bed, but you ainna gonna get it."

What is a Neopolitan virgin?

A girl who can run faster than her brothers.

* * *

Stan Wanderman, the California ladies wear manufacturing mogul, makes merry with this hunk of monkeyshines:

Gabriella and Pearl were talking while sewing dresses in the garment center.

"What happened to that guy you was goin' out with?" inquired Pearl.

"Oh, I dropped him," answered the Italian girl. "He was no gentleman."

"Whatta ya mean?"

"No sooner did we park on a dark road than he put his hand up my thigh."

"Well, that shows interest, anyway."

"No, I was brought up proper," said Gabriella. "Every nice girl knows that with a real gentleman, it's always tits first."

Puchano made a fortune in the wholesale produce business. The older he got, the more money he made, and pretty soon he was keeping broads all over town. Unfortunately, Puchano wasn't much use to any of them.

One day he went to a surgeon and said, "I wanna be castrated."

"You want to be what?"

"Castrated!" said the Italian. "My sexual powers are failing."

The doctor hesitated for a moment, but Puchano placed $2,000 on his desk. Next day, the M.D. performed the operation.

A few weeks later Puchano was listening to some of the guys talking down at the produce market.

"Say, Carmine, do you think there's anything to it that if a man gets himself circumcised it improves his sexual performance?"

"Damn it!" muttered Puchano to himself. "*Circumcised*, that's the word I been trying to think of."

Rigamonti was visiting a small town in the Italian alps. After a few lonely nights he began feeling the need for a woman. He asked the local barkeep how to find the ladies of the town.

"We ain't gotta no prostitutes, the Church would never allow it. But the thing-a you want is kept out of sight."

"What I gotta do?" asked Rigamonti.

The bartender explained that up in the mountains were caves. "Go up there at dusk and shout, 'Yoo-oo-hoo,' and if the lady yoo-oo-hoos back, you work out the price. If she's-a busy, you no get an answer."

That evening Rigamonti yoo-hoo'd his way from cave to cave, but without luck. He finally decided to go back and get drunk, but at the foot of the mountain he found a fresh cave.

"Yoo-hoo, yoo-hoo," he shouted.

"Yoo-hoo, yoo-hoo-oo-oo-oo," came back so clearly.

He rushed into the cave and was killed by a train.

"*Hoo-hoo! Hoo-hoo-hoo-hoo!*"

Da Vita was bicycling past a house on a narrow Philadelphia street when a used condom was thrown out of an upper window and hit him smack in the eye.

This caused him to fall off the bike. He was very angry. He knocked at the front door of the house and a man said, "Yes?"

"Who's-a upstairs where that light is?"

"My daughter."

"And who's-a with her?"

"My future son-in-law."

"I thought-a you'd like-a to know that you future grandson has just-a been thrown out-a da window."

* * *

MARRIAGE ITALIAN STYLE

What is the first thing they do at Italian weddings after the priest says, "With this ring I thee wed?"

They take the handcuffs off the groom.

* * *

At an Italian wedding, how can you tell the difference between members of the Mafia and the musicians?

The musicians are the ones without the violin cases.

* * *

Who are the six most important people at an Italian wedding?

The priest. the bride, the groom, and their three kids.

Did you hear about the Italian girl who believed in long engagements?

She was pregnant six months before she got married.

* * *

After the marriage ceremony of her only daughter, Mrs. Del Monte took the girl aside and gave her advice about the first night.

"What-a happens in-a da bedroom is-a very important," said the mother. "Tonight, you put on-a lots-a perfume. Sprinkle-a powder on-a da bed. Wear a real-a flimsy night-a-gown. You be ready when you man-a comes to get-a you!"

"Mama!" said the girl, "I know how to screw! How do you make lasagna?"

* * *

What do two flamingos do when they get married?

They put two cast iron Italians out on their front lawn.

For a wedding present, Sandicchi gave his son Aldo $200. Two weeks later he asked him, "What you do with-a the money?"

"I bought a wristwatch, Papa!" answered the boy.

"*Stupido!*" cried his father. "You should-a bought a rifle!"

"A rifle? What for?"

"Suppose-a some day you come-a home an-a find a man-a sleepin'-a wid you wife," explained Sandicchi. "What-a you gonna do? Wake him-a up and tell-a him what-a time it is?"

* * *

Did you hear about the Italian bride who was murdered on her honeymoon?

On the first night she kneeled beside the bed and said, "Now I lay me down to sleep!"

* * *

How do you know who's the bride at an Italian wedding?

She's the one who is pregnant.

Three weeks after arriving in America, Marcelli telephoned his mother in Rome.

"*Mama mia!*" he bellowed excitedly. "I'm-a so happy. I'm-a gonna marry an-a American-a girl!"

"No! No!" pleaded his mother. "American-a girl is-a no good. She's a bad-a cook. She's-a bad in-a the bed. And if you have-a the fight, she's-a gonna call you 'Wop'!"

Despite his mother's pleas, Marcelli married the girl and a month later again phoned his mother.

"Mama! Mama! You all-a wrong!" shouted the Italian. "She's a great-a cook! She's a wonderful in-a the bed! And Mama, the only time she's-a call-a me 'Wop' is when I call-a her 'Coon'!"

*   *   *

What do you call an Italian who marries a Negro?

A social climber.

*   *   *

What's the last thing they do at an Italian wedding?

Flush the punch bowl.

Young Mazzilli wasn't getting along too well with his wife. One night he threw a big party and invited all his friends.

At the beginning everyone sat around just making small talk. But as the evening progressed, people started to couple off and find cozy corners.

Soon, the lights were dimmed, and moans of love and passion could be heard. Mazzilli began looking for his wife, but couldn't find her.

After searching everywhere in the apartment, he stepped into the kitchen and there she was, sitting on the sink, her legs in passionate embrace around Vince, one of his friends.

"Your wife and I love each other," stammered Vince, "and we want to get married. Can you forgive me for taking her away?"

"Hey," smiled the husband, "that's what this party was for!"

* * *

Did you hear about the old Italian who married a young girl acrobat so that she could do a handstand while he dropped it in?

"My daughter Emilla just-a got married."

"I heard she's-a marry a soldier."

"Atsa right. And she's-a such a good girl. She's-a write-a to the army for her husband's-a favorite food recipes."

* * *

DeMarco was very upset over Pietro, his 20-year-old son. It seems the boy masturbated several times a day.

"Why you no get marriage?" asked the father.

So Pietro found himself a real pretty girl from the neighborhood. A short time later, Zottola found his son down in the cellar, once again wacking off.

"Holy mackerels!" cried DeMarco. "I thought-a this would all stop, now that you gotta marriage to Rosaria."

"But Papa!" said Pietro. "the poor girl—her little arm gets so tired!"

* * *

Chuck and Angie had just been married and were in the back of a taxi heading for the airport. The groom tried to unbutton her blouse, but she fought him off. He tried again up her leg.

"Hey, lay off that stuff," protested the Italian girl. "I'm a respectable married woman now."

* * *

Mario and Adriena left on their honeymoon. She went up to bed first to get ready, and he followed soon afterwards. He found her stark naked in the bedroom, except for a baseball cap on her head.

"Hey," he said, "you gone nuts?"

"No, I'm just doing what my mother told me to."

"What's that?"

"She said, if I wanna keep my husband's interest I should never let him see me completely naked."

* * *

When is an Italian wedding considered to be really classy?

When the organ grinder brings *two* monkeys.

Mrs. Panuzzi met Mrs. Zurigo, the organ grinder's wife, at the grocery store. "You husband's-a monkey died?" asked Mrs. Panuzzi.

"Yeah," said Mrs. Zurigo.

"Atsa too bad. I heard he had-a da monkey's glands-a put in."

"Yeah."

"How's he doin'?"

"I donna know!" answered Mrs. Zurigo. "He's a still up in-a chandelier eating-a peanuts."

* * *

Condolli decided to become an organ grinder and brought home a monkey to the one room in which he and his wife lived.

"What-a will he eat?" asked Mrs. Condolli.

"The same food as-a we do," says the Italian.

"And where's he gonna sleep?"

"In-a da bed wid us."

"And what about-a the smell?"

"If I could-a get used to it, so could-a he!"

A smart New York career girl married Stefano, a handsome young Italian farmer. She wasn't too happy with his social manner and started trying to improve him immediately. Throughout the wedding reception she continuously corrected his mistakes, telling him what to say, which knife to use at the table, and how to pass the butter. Finally, the celebrations were over, and they were in bed at last.

Stefano fidgeted between the sheets, unsure of himself, but finally he turned toward his new wife and stuttered, "Could you pass the pussy, please?"

* * *

Joey was sitting in his Bronx living room reading the newspaper when his wife Carla came over and slapped him.

"What was that for?" asked the husband.

"That's for being a lousy lover."

A little while later, Joey went over to where his wife was sitting watching TV and he gave her a whack in the mouth.

"What was that for?" she shouted.

"For knowin' the difference."

Brian Rouff, the gifted young comedy writer, came up with this cackler:

Guido and his wife, Teresa, set up shop on the city sidewalk. Guido ground the hand organ, Teresa sang, and their monkey, Sazeech, danced around waving a tin cup.

When a crowd had gathered, Guido said, "Let's have-a some coins for Sazeech. He's-a the smartest-a monkey on-a this earth. He can-a dance and-a juggle and do a han-a-stan'—almost-a anything a human can-a do"

"Say," shouted a man in the crowd, "if the chimp's so smart, how come you keep him on a leash?"

"Ask-a my wife," replied Guido. "She's-a the one who taught-a him to monkey around!"

"She taught-a him to monkey around!"

Spinetti and Fazio were having a glass of vino. "Ever see an ice cube with a hole in it?" asked Spinetti.

"Yeah," replied Fazio, "I was married to one for twenty years."

* * *

The Salvinis were married for years. One night while they were making love, he asked, "Dear, am I hurting you?"

"No," she replied, "why do you ask?"

"You moved," he replied.

* * *

Rosanna met Sean O'Shaugnessy at a singles dance. The Italian girl was strongly attracted to the Irishman and soon they were married.

On the first night of their honeymoon, Rosanna slipped into her sexy mini-night-gown and crawled into bed. But Sean settled down on a chair and began to read the newspaper.

When she asked him why he wasn't going to make love to her, Sean said, "Because it's Lent!"

"You're kidding!" said the Italian girl, "To who—and for how long?"

What is the difference between an Italian mother-in-law and an elephant?
About fifty pounds.

*   *   *

Did you hear about the Italian housewife who is so fat that when she takes a bath they have to grease the sides of the tub?

*   *   *

Ken Bonnett, Wyoming's champion home builder, tells about Nottolini sitting on the front steps weeping bitterly.

"What's-a matta for you?" asked his neighbor Cozzi.

"La Gotta's wife-a just-a die," said Nottolini, wiping at his tears.

"So what?" said his neighbor. "She was-a no relative of yours."

"I know that," said Nottolini. "It's-a just-a that everybody seems-a to have-a good luck but-a me!"

Pacchelli's wife died and the house rang with his cries of lament. He wailed and moaned, and yet the next day his brother found him in bed making love to the housemaid.

"What's-a matta wid you?" shouted his brother. "You wife is-a no even buried-a twenty-four hours!"

"In my grief," said Pacchelli, "how should-a I know what I'm-a doin'?"

*   *   *

Maria Neglia, the lovely violin virtuoso, gets screams with this story in between her show-stopping artistry:

Laudonio's wife had just died and he was hysterical at the graveside. He kept tearing at his hair and yelling, "What-a am I gonna do? What-a am I gonna do?"

Father Farrugia gently took Laudonio's arm and tried to console him. "My son, you have suffered a terrible loss, but you'll get over it in time," he said, leading Laudonio away from the cemetery.

"Oh, what-a am I gonna do?" wailed Laudonio "What-a am I gonna do?"

"You'll get over your grief," said the parish priest. "In a year or two you'll find some young woman, marry her, and everything will be fine."

"Father, I know-a all that!" said the Italian, "but what-a am I gonna do *tonight*!?"

* * *

LaGatta was sentenced to jail for having intercourse with his wife's body a few hours after her death.

"Do you have anything to say in your own defense?" asked the judge.

"Honest, mista You Honor," replied the Italian. "I didna know she was-a dead. She's-a been like-a that for the last-a twenty years!"

* * *

The Feduzzis were having a big fight. "We're married only six months and already you got yourself a mistress," shouted Mrs. Feduzzi hysterically.

"Honest, doll," said her husband, "I ain't got no other broad. You're the only one!"

"Don't lie to me, you bastard!" screamed the wife. "This week alone you washed your feet three times already!"

After answering the phone Ralph returned to the living room where his sexy wife lay sprawled on the couch. "Who was that on the phone?" she asked.

"I don't know," answered Ralph. "It's the third time tonight. The guy must think I'm in the coast guard."

"Why?"

"He keeps calling up and askin' if the coast is clear."

* * *

Patsy and his buddy Dario were strolling along a Chicago street. After a long silence Patsy said, "Eh, what's eatin' you?"

"Aah, somethin's been botherin' me for days," said Dario. "Maybe it ain't none of my business, but you and me've been buddies for years and I just gotta tell ya."

"Go 'head, spill it!" said Patsy.

"Last Saturday night I was in a whorehouse and who do I see there, but your wife, Christine. I hate to say it, Pal, but Christine's a prostitute!"

"Aah, go'wan. Christine ain't no prostitute," answered Patsy. "She's just a substitute. She's only there on weekends!"

Filici had stomach trouble, so he consulted a doctor. "How often do you make love?" asked the M.D.

"Monday, Wednesday, and Friday," he replied.

"That may be a little too much for you at your age," said the M.D. "You'll have to cut out Wednesdays!"

"I can't," said the Italian, "that's the only night I come home!"

* * *

Did you hear about the Italian who wanted to keep his wife's cold from going from her head to her chest?

He tied a knot in her throat.

* * *

Mrs. Carbotti went to the doctor complaining of fatigue. After the examination, the M.D. decided she needed a rest.

"Can you stop having relations with your husband for about three weeks?" he asked.

"Sure," she replied, "I got two boyfriends who can take care-a me for that long!"

Bill Pine, the clever California record cover creator, contributed this dash of whimsy:

Lorenzo staggered home filled with vino and his wife wouldn't let him in the house. "Hey, Rosa," he shouted from below their window. "If you donna let me in, I'm-a gonna tell everybody I slept-a with you before we got married."

"Go ahead," yelled back his spouse. "And I'm-a gonna tell them you-a weren't the first-a one!"

"You weren't the first-a one!"

Vito and Lloyd were eating their lunch. Vito confided that his sex life wasn't too good because his wife, Rosa, had become indifferent.

"It's technique," said Lloyd. "Women like to have sweet nothings whispered in their ears. You ever call her endearing names?"

"Naw! I just call her by her name, Rosa."

"It's worth a try," assured Lloyd.

That evening Vito walked into the kitchen and called out, "And how is my sweet Rambler Rose tonight?"

Rosa looked at him suspiciously and said, "You gone nuts or sumpin?"

Next day, Vito reported no progress, but Lloyd suggested he try again. That night, again Vito burst into the kitchen and blurted out, "And how is my sweet Rambler Rose this evening?"

Rosa picked up the rolling pin that she was using and was about to whack him.

"Hey! Why you gonna hit me?"

"Because," she screeched, "I look up Rambler Rose in my garden book and it says, 'Not good in a bed but great against a wall!...'"

Mrs. O'Brien and Mrs. Taglioni were sipping coffee. "Good heavens," moaned Mrs. O'Brien. "Look out the window! Here comes my husband with a dozen roses!"

"What's-a wrong with-a dozen roses?" asked the Italian woman.

"Are you kidding?" said the Irish woman. "Me legs'll be spread apart all weekend now!"

"What's-a matta?" asked Mrs. Taglioni. "You no gotta da vase?"

* * *

The psychiatrist asked Zanolli, "Have you ever committed sodomy?"

"No, sir," said the Italian, "One-a wife is enough-a for me!"

* * *

"Hey, Lucatelli, how you manage to get along so good with your wife?"

"I always tell her the truth, even if I have to lie a little."

Manetti, the mechanic, woke up one morning with a black eye.

"What happened?" he asked his wife.

"While you were sleeping," she explained, "you reached over and felt my arms and said, 'What a smooth finish.' Then you reached over further and said, 'What perfect headlights.' Then you reached down further and said, 'Who left the garage door open?' And that's when I let you have it!"

* * *

"Who says the Italians don't have birth control devices?"

"We do?"

"Sure. My wife just takes off her makeup."

* * *

"How's your wife, Ralphie?"

"Better than nothing!"

Banzini's wife was expecting, and he was pacing up and down outside the maternity ward.

At last the nurse came out and said, "Congratulations, you've got a pair of twins!"

"Oh, that's the end of our marriage," said the Italian. "I never thought she fool around wid annoder man."

"That's ridiculous!"

"But, nurse, I only make-a da love once. The other baby no can-a belong-a to me!"

*　　*　　*

Vittorio: You don't deserve a husband like me.

Caterina: I don't deserve sinus trouble either, but I got it.

*　　*　　*

Mrs. Marzanini complained to a lawyer that every time she had relations with her husband it hurt unbearably. "He's big! He's like a horse," she added.

"In that case," said the attorney, "the best thing you can do is to file your petition."

"Oh, no! Let him sandpaper his..."

Rampazzo missed a day at work and O'Riley, the foreman, wanted an explanation. "Where've you been?" he asked.

"It was-a my wife, she gave-a birth to a wheelbarrow."

"If you can't do any better than that," said the foreman, "I'm gonna have to let you go."

"I think-a I got it-a wrong," said Rampazzo. "My wife she's in-a bed havin' a pushchair."

"That's it wise guy!" shouted O'Riley. "You're fired!"

Rampazzo went home and said, "Hey missus, what-a was wrong-a with you yesterday?"

"I told-a you, I had a miscarriage!"

"Oh, I knew it was-a something with-a wheels on."

* * *

Did you hear about the Italian who bought a union suit because his wife was having labor pains?

Testatori's wife was having so many children the doctor said to him, "You wear a sheath. As long as you wear it, your wife cannot conceive."

However, she soon became pregnant again, and the doctor was furious. He had Testatori in, and asked him what happened.

"I swear I wear it," said the Italian. "I no take it off."

"Then how the hell did your wife conceive?"

"After one-a week I have-a to pee so bad, I cut-a the end off."

* * *

Constanza consulted his doctor because his wife was having far too many children. The doctor gave him a condom and said to follow the instructions and all would be well.

A month later the man was back saying his wife was pregnant again.

"Did you follow the instructions?"

"Docta, it said: 'Stretch-a over da organ before innercourse.' But we no gotta da organ, so I stretch it over the piano."

Gene Panoz, the lovable director of Pittsburgh's Moose Club # 28, cracks up customers with this cajoler:

Olivo, a soldier in the days of ancient Rome, was called off to war. Fearing for the safety of his beautiful young wife, he locked her in armor from the waist down and gave the key to his best friend.

"If I do not return in six months," said the warrior, "Use the key. To you, and only you, do I entrust it!"

He galloped off to battle.

Olivo had only gone five miles when he heard hoof beats behind him. Through a cloud of dust appeared his closest friend who shouted excitedly, "Stop! You gave me the wrong key!"

"Stop! You gave me the wrong key!"

Did you hear about the Italian guy who divorced his wife because she was giving car salesmen demonstration rides?

* * *

ANCIENT PALERMO PROVERB

*An Italian wife will forgive and forget
But she'll never forget what she forgave*

* * *

Perazzi and Lamano were sitting on a bench in a New York park. "Hey," said Perazzi, "do you like-a big-a fat woman with a long-a straggly hair?"

"No," said Lamano.

"You like-a woman with a garlic comin' from her mouth all-a the time?"

"No!" said his friend.

"You like a woman with a big, thick-a hips and-a varicose-a veins?"

"No!" answered his pal.

"Then why you keep-a screwin' my wife?"

It was Friday afternoon, and the foreman told Pitore he'd have to work overtime, so Pitore asked his friend Gondolfo to stop at the house and tell his wife.

Gondolfo knocked on the door and said to Mrs. Pitore, "You old man ain't coming home until late. How 'bout we go upstairs and make-a the screw."

The young Mrs. Pitore was shocked and refused fiercely.

"I give-a you fifty bucks!"

"How dare you?"

"One hundred dollars, then."

"Er, well no, it wouldn't hardly be right, would it?"

"Come on, two hundred dollars; just for half an hour on the bed, and Pitore'll never find out!"

She needed no more persuading, but led him to the bedroom, took the money, and gave Gondolfo the time of his life.

When the husband came home late, he said, "Did my friend Gondolfo tell-a you I be workin' over?"

"Yeah, he was here for a minute."

"And I hope-a he gave you my wages like-a I told him."

* * *

VATICAN VARIETIES

What is the Pope's phone number?
Et cum spiri 220.

*   *   *

The Pope was reading in his Vatican sanctuary when suddenly he was called to the telephone.

"This is-a Father Balducci in New York," said the voice. "Your Holiness, I think that Jesus Christ is walking down the middle of Fifth Avenue. What should I do?"

"Look-a busy!" replied the Pontiff.

The Pope lay dying. His doctor called the cardinals together and announced, "We can only save his life with a heart transplant."

"We must tell the people," said one of the cardinals. "Perhaps a donor will volunteer to give his heart for the Pontiff."

The announcement was made and thousands gathered beneath the Pope's balcony shouting, "Take-a my heart! Take-a my heart!"

The cardinals now had to decide on the person who would donate his heart to the Holy Father. "We'll drop a feather from His Holiness's hat," said the head Cardinal. "Whoever it lands upon will be the lucky person."

The feather floated down from the balcony. From the multitudes below came, "Take-a my heart! *(Blowing)* Whew! Take-a my heart! *(Blowing)* Whew!"

* * *

Father Navazio and Father Canulli were sitting in a Vatican courtyard chatting.

"Do you think the Pope will ever allow priests to marry?" asked Father Navazio.

"It won't happen in our time," replied Father Canulli. "Maybe in our children's!"

* * *

The Pope stood before a hushed crowd of attentive villagers, and spoke to them: "You must not use-a the Pill!"

A young, good-looking signorina stepped forward and said, "Look, you no play-a da game, you no make-a da rules!"

* * *

Miglio and Marini were watching a jet fly overhead. "Hey, atsa the Pope up-a there!" declared Miglio.

"How you know that?" asked Marini.

"Atsa easy," replied the first Italian. "The airplane-a say TWA. Top-a Wop Aboard."

* * *

Rocchi stood before the parish priest. "Fatha, before I die I'm-a gonna convert to-a be a Protestant."

"But why would you do that?" asked the astonished clergyman.

"Well," said Rocchi, "you no wanna lose a Catholic when I go, do you?"

A few days after the new Pope had been elected, Cardinal Sicola had dinner with an old friend, Rabbi Finkalari.

They chatted about many things and the Rabbi noticed that Cardinal Sicola seemed rather dejected. "Dear friend," said the Rabbi. "You seem disturbed. Is it anything you care to discuss with me?"

"You know, I did not labor under any illusion that I might be elected. I just never dreamed I was so unpopular as not to have received even one vote!"

"My dear Cardinal," consoled the Rabbi. "Dismiss such thoughts from your mind. You are held in very high esteem by your colleagues. I know what must have been on their minds. Each one undoubtedly figured that if you were elected, it would sound demeaning to call you Pope-Sicola!"

* * *

Carmella went to confession and told the priest that she had been having an affair with a married man.

"But this is the tenth time you have told me about this," remonstrated the priest.

"I know. Father." said the woman, "but I like to talk about it."

An Italian painter named Giotto
Seduced a nun in a grotto
  The result of his crime
  Was two boys at one time.
"Give your sons to the church," was his
  motto.

* * *

Zarillo and Marchetti were passing time after their hero sandwich lunch. "Hey," said Zarillo, "did you know it took Michelangelo more than twenty years to paint the dome of the Sistine Chapel?"

"Yeah?" said Marchetti. "Well, he'd-a done it a lot faster if he'd-a got himself a paint roller!"

* * *

Did you hear about the Italian who thought the St. Louis Cardinals were appointed by the Pope?

* * *

At a Mafia funeral how can you tell the difference between members of the Mafia and the priest?

The priest is the one without the white tie.

Patricia Matthews, America's newest best-selling romance novelist, conjured up this cutie:

Michelangelo was painting the ceiling of the Sistine Chapel. He was getting tired lying on his back and in rolling over noticed old Mrs. Iannilli praying down in the chapel.

He sat at the edge of the scaffold and shouted, "I am Jesus Christ! I am Jesus Christ! Listen to me and I will perform miracles!"

The Italian lady looked up clasping her rosary and answered back, "Shut up-a you mouth! I'm-a talk-a to you mother!"

"Shut up-a you face. I'm-a talk-a to
you mother!"

Nastari had worked in a lumberyard for fifteen years. During all that time, he never went to church. He lived high on the hog stealing lumber and selling it to pay for his excesses.

At last, his conscience began to bother him. He decided to repent and went to confession.

"Fatha," he wailed, "I been-a away from-a the church for more than-a fifteen years. And worse than that, I been-a stealing lumber to pay for my havin' a good-a times!"

"How much lumber have you stolen?" asked the priest.

"I took-a the lumber every day for fifteen years."

"Stolen lumber every day for fifteen years! My son, can you make a novena?"

"If you gotta da plans, Fatha, I gotta da lumber!"

*　*　*

Father Padovani had been preaching about sex and morality to his Little Italy congregation.

"Sex is-a dirty!" he shouted. "I wanna

see only good-a girls today. I wanna every virgin in-a church to-a stand up."

Not a soul in a pew moved. Then after a long pause, a sexy-looking blonde holding an infant in her arms got to her feet.

"Virgins is-a what I want!" said the outraged *padre.*

"Hey, Father," she asked, "you expect a two-month-old baby to stand by herself?"

* * *

The nuns ran an orphanage in Northern Italy. One day the Mother Superior summoned t her office three well-endowed teenagers who were leaving.

"Girls, you're all going out into the big sinful world, and I must warn you against certain men," she said. "There are men who will buy you drinks, take you to a room, undress you, and do unspeakable things to you. Then they give you twenty or thirty dollars and you're sent away, ruined!"

"Excuse me, Reverend Mother," said the boldest one, "did you say these wicked men do this to us and give us thirty dollars?"

"Yes, dear child, why do you ask?"

"Well, the priests only give us apples."

Some nuns were getting very restless. The weather was very hot, and quarreling was breaking out.

The Mother Superior called them together and demanded to know what was the matter.

A novice, Sister Anna Lucia, said, "What this place needs is some healthy males."

The Reverend Mother was shocked. "She's right," cried Sister Maria Cristina, "it's only human nature, isn't it?"

"Very well then," said the Mother Superior, "since it's such hot weather I will issue you all with candles, and you have my dispensation to comfort yourselves with them."

"They're no good, we've tried them," cried several voices.

"When I was young they were all right," said the Reverend Mother. "What's the objection?"

"Well," said Sister Maria Cristina. "You get tired of the same thing wick in and wick out!"

The Mother Superior of the convent awoke in a happy mood, dressed, and set off to visit her flock.

"Good morning, Sister Augusta. God bless you! Are you happy at your work?"

"Yes, Reverend Mother, but I'm sorry to see you got out of bed on the wrong side this morning."

The Mother Superior ignored the remark and passed on to another nun.

"Good morning, Sister Giorgina. You look pleased with yourself."

"I am, Reverend Mother. But it's a pity you got out of bed on the wrong side today!"

The Mother Superior, greatly puzzled, moved on to a young novice. "Tell me, little sister, do you also feel I got out of bed on the wrong side?"

"I'm afraid so!" said the nun.

"But why? Am I not as happy as a songbird, and pleasant to you all?"

"Yes, Mother, but you're wearing Father Vincenza's house slippers."

* * *

GARLIC GIGGLES

Why does an Italian have a hole in his pants pocket?
So he can count to six.

*   *   *

How do you circumcise an Italian?
Wop!

*   *   *

Did you hear about the Italian girl who was doing fine at her new job at the sanitary napkin factory until the foreman found her putting get well cards in each carton?

How can you tell an Italian funeral?
The first six garbage trucks have their lights on.

*   *   *

What is the national bird of Italy?
The stool pigeon.

*   *   *

Why can't an Italian take a shower?
Because oil and water don't mix.

*   *   *

How do you kill an Italian when he's drinking?
Close the toilet seat on him.

*   *   *

DeLuca walked into the neighborhood poolroom flashing a shiny new pinkie ring.

"Hey," asked one of his buddies, "that's some diamond you got there. Is it real?"

"If it ain't," replied DeLuca, "I been cheated outa five bucks."

Did you hear about the Hollywood producer who wanted to give a new Italian actress a tremendous build-up—but nature beat him to it?

* * *

What is the main difference between Italian movie starlets and French movie starlets?

French starlets don't have hair on their chests.

* * *

The Hollywood movie producer had recently signed up an Italian actress and was holding a press conference.

"When will she make her first picture?" asked the reporter.

"She no speak-a English so good. I'm-a gonna learn her how."

* * *

Did you hear about the Italian starlet who wears black panties labeled: MADE IN HOLLYWOOD—BY ALMOST EVERBODY.

Mrs. Pacelli: I'm-a disgusted.
Neighbor: Why?
Mrs. Pacelli: I step-a on-a the scale today, and it say: *One person at a time, please!*

* * *

De Angelo was having a tough time trying to decide what costume he should wear to the masquerade party. Finally, after much thought, he stole a pair of his mother-in-law's bloomers—and went as a tent.

* * *

Did you hear about the Italian girl who has a terrible time in the morning?

She's so fat, she rocks herself to sleep trying to get up.

* * *

Why do Italians paint their trash cans orange and blue?

So their mothers will think they're going to Howard Johnson's.

Rocco and Tony, two of the "boys," were preparing a little action.

"Foist, we knock off the Toid National Bank," said Rocco. "Then we heist the Fort National Bank, then we rob the Sixth National Bank."

"Wait a minute," said Tony, "you left out the Fifth National Bank."

"Dat joint we lay off!" said Rocco. "Dat's where I keep all *my* dough!"

*   *   *

Petrucci, the burglar, broke into a store five times. "But I stole only one dress!" he protested as he confessed.

"How can that be?" asked the detective.

"I wanted to get a dress for my girlfriend, but she kept making me take it back!"

*   *   *

Did you hear about the new Italian car called the Mafia?

It's got a hood under the hood. And it's got a beautiful body—in the trunk.

A tourist walked into Kintie's Cannibal Caterers, a posh restaurant in Africa, and said, "What's good on the menu today?"

"Well, we got sauteed Frenchman for $3.95!" said the waiter.

"What else!" asked the customer.

"You can have roast breast of Englishman for $5.95."

"Anything else?"

"Yes, we have fried Italian at $16.50!"

"How come that's so much more expensive?" asked the tourist.

"You know how tough it is to clean one of them?" replied the waiter.

Dazzini and Jotta were having an argument. "When it comes-a to Chianti I'm-a da expert!" claimed Dazzini.

"What makes you so smart?" asked Jotta.

"You just-a gimme a glass of vino and I not only name-a da year it was-a made but I tell-a you who jump on-a da grapes."

* * *

Did you hear about the Italian who makes his own sparkling burgundy?

He uses two bottles of red wine and a bicycle pump.

* * *

The doctor wanted to know what Romani could have eaten to necessitate the use of a stomach pump.

"I dunno, Doc," said Romani. "I only had a light between-meal snack: six hamburgers, without no relish or nothin', a couple dozen jelly doughnuts, and three, four cups-a Java."

"I thought so," said the physician. "Over indulgence!"

"Naw! Over in Jersey!"

Henry Heller, Indianapolis's top insurance agent, tells about the captain of an Al Italia jet who was speaking over the intercom to his passengers:

"Folksa, I got-a some good news and-a some bad news. First-a, the bad news! We're lost!

"Now the good-a news! We're making excellent time!"

* * *

Why did Gionetti lose his job as an elevator operator?
He couldn't learn the route.

* * *

Pierre and Domenico were in the woods hunting together when suddenly a voluptuous blonde raced across their path, totally nude.

"Oh, *mon Dieu!*" cried the Frenchman, smacking his lips, "would I like to eat that?"
So the Italian shot her.

Did you hear about Lintozzi spending two weeks in a revolving door—looking for a doorknob?

* * *

How would you describe six Italians in a circle?
A dope ring.

* * *

Why are the New York City garbage trucks painted bright yellow?
So the Italians can use them for summer bungalows.

* * *

In order to get a job with the railroad, Cinelli had to pass a test. "Suppose two trains were heading for each other at one hundred miles per hour on the same track," asked the personnel manager, "What would you do?"
"I take-a the red flag and wave-a them to a stop," Cinelli answered.
"But you don't have a red flag!" pointed out the man.

"Then I'm-a take the switch-a iron and change-a the tracks!"

"You don't have a switch iron either!"

"Well, in that-a case," said the Italian, "I'm-a gonna call up-a my wife Benita!"

"What's your wife got to do with two trains coming at each other at one hundred miles an hour?" asked the personnel manager.

"I tell-a her to come down—cause she's-a gonna see the biggest-a smash up in da whole world!"

* * *

Did you hear about the Mafia don who had his insurance canceled because it was for straight life?

* * *

Why won't they take Italians in the paratroopers?

They can't count to ten.

* * *

What is the best thing about Italy?

The road over the border to Switzerland.

Renaldo returned to Italy to see his relatives. One day he tried to ride his uncle's horse.

"Giddy-up! Giddy-up!" he said to the animal. But it did not move.

"Hey!" he said to his relative. "Why this thing-a no move-a?"

"You no say 'Giddy-up,'" said his uncle. "You gotta say *'Mama mia'* to make-a him go and *'mangiare'* to make him stop!"

"Mama mia!" he yelled, and the horse galloped off into a clearing. Ahead was a steep cliff and Renaldo noticed it almost too late. He pulled back on the reins and screamed *"Mangiare!!!"*

The horse came to a screeching halt at the edge of the cliff. Looking down and then up at the sky, Renaldo whispered, *"Mama mia!!"*

"Mama mia!"

John Cacavacas, the award-winning Hollywood music composer, is also a gourmet cook with a great sense of humor:

"French fries are really very good but Italian fries are just as tasty. You should try them. First, you take two quarts of motor oil . . ."

* * *

THE WONDER OF ITALY

How one country could turn out such small cars and such big women

* * *

The phone awoke Gallitti at three o'clock in the morning. It was his friend Banaldi calling long distance from Florida.

"What's-a matta?" asked Gallitti, "you in-a trouble?"

"No," said Banaldi.

"What-a you want?"

"Nothing!"

"Then why you call-a me in the middle of-a the night?"

"Because," said his friend, "the rates is-a cheaper!"

How do you break an Italian's finger?
You punch him in the nose.

* * *

Did you hear about the Italian bookies who are finally getting even?
Last week they closed two police stations.

* * *

Why did people at the World's Fair run around searching for manhole covers?
They were looking for the entrance to the Italian Pavilion.

* * *

Do you know why Italians can't surf?
'Cause they're wop-sided.

* * *

Mrs. Columbus watched her husband get ready to ship off. "What do you mean, Christopher," she said, "you goin' on a West Indies cruise without me!"

Comedian Jeremy Vernon says, "Two great things have come out of Italy in the last twenty years and Sophia Loren has both of them."

*   *   *

AUTOMOTIVE NEWS FLASH

Italy has produced a new car called the "Fiasco." It uses no fuel. You just put lasagna in the tank. Then linguini with clam sauce and then some ravioli alla marinara. By the time it gets to the engine it's pure gas.

*   *   *

A housewife picked out three small tomatoes at D'Agostino's vegetable market and was told they were 75 cents.

"Seventy-five cents for these tiny tomatoes?" she exclaimed. "Well, you can just take them and you know what you can do with them!"

"I can't-a lady!" replied D'Agostino. "There's-a ninety-five cent-a cucumber already there!"

Why did Columbus come to America?
He was trying to get away from Italy.

* * *

A recently arrived Sicilian was being questioned by the regulars at the neighborhood bar. "Hey, Manelli," one of them yelled. "Tell us the truth. How do you like America?"

"Ah," answered the little immigrant smilingly, "it's-a fine place. One thing only I donna understan'. You got-a here a fat man, everybody call-a him 'Tiny.' A bald-a headed man, he's-a call 'Curly.' Me, I'm-a here two monthe, ain't-a had no woman, me they call a f——g Guinea!"

* * *

Not long ago, in a sociology class, a serious student asked the professor why the early Mafia was known as the Black Hand.

"I don't know!" said the professor. "Their feet were just as dirty."

Did you hear that Italy bought tons of sand from the Arabs?

They're going to dig for their own oil.

*　　*　　*

What do you have when you find 12 Italians on your front lawn?

Fertilizer.

*　　*　　*

"Italians were not involved in Watergate."

"What about John Sirica?"

"He was a good guy. But if Italians were in on it there never would have been a Watergate. Because there never would have been any witnesses."

*　　*　　*

How do the women in Rome really know they're getting along in years?

When their shoes pinch them more than men do.

Mariotti and Figlio made a pact that the one who died first would try to make contact with the one left on earth. Mariotti was the first to go, and for months Figlio waited in vain for a word or a sign.

One day, however, as he was walking down a side street, he heard, "Figlio, my friend! It's-a Mariotti." He looked in every direction, but the only living thing in sight was a spindly, underfed horse, hitched to a dilapidated icewagon.

"Yeah," said the horse sadly, "it's-a me, Mariotti. Live as long as you can, Figlio, for see what happens when you die! I belong to this pig Pasquali. He beats me, starves me, and makes me lug this icewagon around sixteen hours a day!"

"But you can talk," bellowed Figlio. "Why you no raise hell with Pasquali."

"Shhh," said Mariotti. "For God's sake, no let-a him know I can-a talk. He'll have me hollering 'Ice!' "

* * *

Did you hear about the Italian woman who is so fat she uses inner tubes for garters?

Peter Alpert, the prominent Los Angeles attorney, loves this lighthearted lampoon:

A small plane was flying over Italy. As it passed over the bay of Naples, the pilot said to his passenger, "Have you ever heard the expression, 'See Naples and die?'"

"Yes, I have, why?" answered the passenger.

"Well, take a good-a look," said the pilot. "The propeller just-a fell off."

"The propeller just-a fell off."

Why don't they allow Italians to swim in the Hudson River?

They would leave a ring on the shore-line.

*   *   *

NEWS FLASH

Italian inventors have just reached a new peak in their legendary efficiency. A group of scientists working for several years twenty-four hours a day have just invented a pencil with an eraser at both ends.

*   *   *

What is Italian matching luggage?

Two shopping bags from the Safeway.

*   *   *

Recently an Italian convict filed a brief with the court charging that he was being subjected to cruel and unusual punishment. The warden had ordered him to take a shower.

Pete and his girl, Vittoria, were on the couch watching an old Gene Autry movie on TV. As Gene rode through a pass, Pete said, "I'll bet you a screw his horse steps in a gopher hole and falls!"

"Okay," said Vittoria, "you're on!"

Sure enough, the horse stumbled.

After the bet was paid in full, Pete said, "I oughta tell you, I saw the movie before. That's how I knew."

"So did I," said the Italian girl, "but I didn't think a horse would be dumb enough to fall in the same hole twice!"

* * *

Did you hear about the Italian girl who was so fat she had to put her make-up on with a paint roller?

* * *

In Italy, the "high-priced spread" most in demand is axle grease.

* * *

Why does time go so fast in Italy?

Because every time you look around another Dago's by.

What is the best way to grease a Ferrari?

Run over an Italian.

* * *

Why don't they kill flies in Italy?
'Cause it's the national bird.

* * *

How can the police tell when a house had been burglarized by an Italian?

When the toilet seat is up and the cat is pregnant.

* * *

Why don't Italians have pimples?
Because they slide off their faces!

* * *

An American driving through Italy stopped in a small town and asked Lallini and Angelo if they knew where the spaghetti factory was.

"There's-a no spaghetti factory around here," answered Lallini.

After the American drove off, Angelo

said, "Maybe he's-a mean the macaroni factory?"

"Could be," said Lallini. "Let's-a catch him."

They yelled loudly after the traveler, who heard them and stopped the car.

As they got to him, Lallini asked, "Maybe it's-a the macaroni factory you look-a for?"

"Well, now, perhaps it is," nodded the driver. "Where is the macaroni factory?"

"Oh," answered both Italians together, "we don't know where that is either."

* * *

SIGN IN A ROME SHOP WINDOW

Don't be mistaken for an American tourist—wear Italian-made clothes

* * *

Copini, the scholar, was asked, "What sank the Titanic?"

"A big ice-a cube!" he replied.

The bailiff called Miss Rizzoli to the witness stand. She whispered to her lawyer, "Must I bare everything?"

"No," he replied, "just cross your legs."

* * *

Why do flies have wings?
So they can beat Italians to the garbage can.

* * *

Did you hear about Triolo watching them catch tuna?
He said, "Isn't it-a wonderful how they can-a squeeze those two hundred pound fish into such-a little-a cans?"

* * *

NEWS FLASH

The Italian government is installing a clock in the Leaning Tower of Pisa.
Reason: What good is it if you have the inclination, but don't have the time?

What is the simplest mechanical operation in the world?

An Italian! There are only two moving parts—his butt and his mouth—and they are interchangeable.

* * *

Why do Italians talk with their hands?

Because they can't stand each other's breath.

* * *

SIGN IN ASTI SPUMANTI WINERY

PREVENT ON-THE-JOB INCIDENTS
LOCK YOUR CHASITY BELT

* * *

Henny Youngman says he dreamed his wife was Sophia Loren: "And all night she kept nagging me in Italian."

* * *

What is a pizza on a stick?

A Wopsickle.

How can you recognize an Italian helicopter?

The small blade goes, *Guinea! Guinea! Guinea!*

And the big blade goes, *Wop! Wop! Wop!*

* * *

Did you hear about the Italian farmer who ran a steam roller across his fields because he wanted to market mashed potatoes?

* * *

Why does an Italian take his kid to the garbage dump?

To give him on-the-job training.

* * *

Singleton and his wife moved to a small town in Italy. After buying a house, he decided to get a horse. In the newspaper, Singleton read that there was a horse for sale cheap. He went to Pacciani the advertiser's home.

"I change-a my mind, mister," said Pacciani, "I no wanna sell my horse. Besides, he no look-a too good."

"You can't do this to me! He looks fine. Now here's the money and let me have the horse!"

"Okay. If you-a want the horse, take him! But I tell you, he no look-a too good!"

Singleton led the horse on to the road and after a few minutes of riding him, he discovered the horse was blind. Singleton grabbed a shotgun and returned to Pacciani's house.

"This horse is blind! I want my money back or I'll shoot you!"

"Hey, mister! What-a you wanna from me? I told you he no-a look-a too good!"

* * *

How does an Italian housewife reply when the sanitation men ask, "Any garbage today?"

She says, "I'll take three bags!"

"*We cater to Polish weddings.*"

No matter where you go in this world you will be sure to find an Italian. After all, somebody has to pick up the garbage.

* * *

What do they call it when an Italian Ph.D. marries a Puerto Rican dishwasher?
Upward mobility.

* * *

After finishing a huge platter of spare ribs, Giuliano, the gigolo, rubbed his grease-spattered fingers through his curly hair.
"Waste not, want not!" he exclaimed.

* * *

Did you hear about the Venetian hooker who liked all American soldiers in Italy, but had trouble taking care of all of them?
She put a wig on her fanny and opened up a second front.

What is the first lesson you receive at an Italian driving school?

How to open a locked car with a bent hanger.

* * *

Olivia was constantly losing boyfriends because of her grandmother. It seems Grandma Micci, wanting to be modern, was always saying the wrong thing.

One day, Olivia's current boyfriend, Bernie, arrived while she was upstairs changing and the old lady began bragging about her granddaughter.

"I think-a Olivia would rather screw than eat," said Grandma Micci. "There ain't a boy around she hasn't-a screwed with. She's even got-a da phonograph-a record to screw by."

Bernie blushed, grabbed his hat, and beat it out the door. Olivia came down and said, "All right, Grandma, what did you say this time?"

"I only say how much-a you like-a to screw!"

"Oh, my God! How many times must I tell you the word is not *screw*—it's *twist*!"

"Look, Captain Columbus—land! We've discovered land!"

"Wonderful! Cable Queen Isabella immediately!"

"But, Captain, the cable hasn't been invented yet!"

"*Mama mia!* Do I have-a to do everything myself?"

*   *   *

Queen Isabella gave three ships to Columbus. He had the stoutest mast she had ever seen.

*   *   *

What is the difference between an umpire and an Italian?

An umpire watches steals and an Italian steals watches.

FROM VENETIAN POLICE RECORDS

Kidnappers grabbed seven-year-old
Niccolo Lucarelli, and two days later
sent him home with the ransom note.
The Lucarellis sent Niccolo back
with the money.

* * *

Miss Adducci, a more than well-endowed young lady, was trying on an extremely low-cut dress. As she looked at herself in the mirror, she asked the saleswoman if she thought the dress was too low-cut.

"Do you have hair on your chest?" asked the saleswoman.

"No," replied the Italian girl.

"Then it's too low-cut!"

* * *

VENETIAN FUNERAL VERSE
Paulo passed away at 69
And we'll all miss him so
Paulo passed away at 69
Marone! What a way to go!

Little Georgio walked into a cocktail lounge and said to the barmaid, "Gimme a double scotch!"

"Hey, kid," she sighed, "you want to get me in trouble?"

"Maybe later, lady! Right now I just wanna drink."

* * *

"DeMarco got married last week and the boys down at the plant all chipped in and got him a wedding present."

"No kiddin'. What'd they give him?"

"A thirteen piece bedroom set—an army cot and a dozen rubbers."

* * *

Coletti the ice man lugged the large block of ice four flights of stairs to his customer's apartment. He set it on the floor of the kitchen and carefully removed the contents of the icebox. He put the ice in, put everything back, and said, "That'll be a dollar, lady."

"I'm afraid I don't have any money," said the woman.

Coletti took the contents out of the icebox, removed the ice and replaced everything. Just as he hoisted the ice on his back and started to leave the woman said, "Please don't take the ice away. How would you like to take it out in trade?"

"I talk it over with-a my partner," answered Coletti.

"Talk it over with your partner!" she shrieked. "For a lousy dollar piece?"

"But lady, this is-a only July," said the Italian, "An' I already screwed away two tons a ice."

Best-Selling Sports Books
from Pinnacle

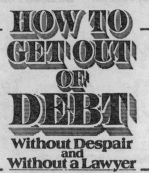